STRONGER

by Barry Tallis

STRONGER: Growing stronger in your faith and your walk with God.

Copyright © 2015 Nourish Ministries, LLC.

PUBLISHED BY: NOURISH MINISTRIES
www.nourishministries.com

All rights reserved. No portion of this book may be reproduced, stored in a retrieval system, or transmitted in any form or by any means - electronic, mechanical, photocopy, recording, or any other - except for brief quotations in printed reviews, without the prior permission of the publisher.

All scripture used is in English Standard Version (ESV). The Holy Bible: English Standard Version. (2001). Wheaton: Standard Bible Society.

ISBN: 978-0-692432-06-8

SPECIAL SALES:
Pastors, churches, and ministry leaders can receive special discounts when purchasing STRONGER resources. For more info, please email info@nourishministries.com

ACKNOWLEDGEMENTS

To my wonderful wife, Dennette. Your unwavering faith and desire to experience more of God, Jesus, and the Holy Spirit has allowed this book to become a reality. You inspire me daily to become stronger. Thank you for your love and your grace.

To my children, your desire to serve Him and grow in Him is so inspiring. The words in this book and the books to come will hopefully create a seed that you will be able to reap a harvest from.

To Pastor Clyde and Cody M., for your servant leadership, faithfulness, and mentorship. Your desire to see His church mature and experience all of the gospel message led me to be filled by the Holy Spirit, and launched me onto a path of growing stronger in my faith and walk with God. Pastor Clyde, your prophetic word from God has come to pass through this book, and the books yet to come.

Thank you to Courtney for reviewing and refining the first draft and to Georgina for your diligence to polish up this manuscript through your excellent editing skills.

CONTENTS

INTRODUCTION	7
STRONGER	12
WHAT GOD WANTS	21
FAITH	32
CHARACTER	47
KNOWLEDGE	59
SELF-CONTROL	70
PERSEVERANCE	78
GODLINESS	91
UNITY	100
LOVE	114
TRAINING PLAN	130

INTRODUCTION

> *"I appeal to you therefore, brothers, by the mercies of God, to present your bodies as a living sacrifice, holy and acceptable to God, which is your spiritual worship. Do not be conformed to this world, but be transformed by the renewal of your mind, that by testing you may discern what is the will of God, what is good and acceptable and perfect"*
> *(Romans 12:1-2)*

I grew up in the Methodist church, and went to church most every Sunday. Every event or group at church I was a part of – from confirmation class to youth group. I was physically invested, but not spiritually invested. I knew about God, but I didn't know Him.

When it came time for me to attend college I consumed myself with the affairs of my own life and stopped going to church. The crazy thing was that I went to college right across the street from the church I grew up in.

In college I made no time for God –attending the typical college parties and only having time for friends and myself. Coincidently my college roommate was a Christian who read his Bible every morning and evening. I suppose he must have been praying for me every single day. Every chance he had, he would share the Gospel story with me and stress to me my need for a Savior. However, my response was always a prideful and angry one when I told him that I didn't need God.

Many years after college I auditioned to be a part of a band. I had always loved music and wanted an opportunity to be a part of a band. Unbeknownst to me, God had a plan for my life before I could even picture it. And auditioning for this band was certainly one of them. My audition was a huge success and I felt at home being there with them.

However, I hadn't realized going into the audition that it was a Christian rock band. After the audition, they asked me about my personal relationship with Jesus and I had no answer for them because I was spiritually barren. At that very moment, I confessed everything and accepted the Lord as my Savior right there on the floor of the studio. A huge weight was immediately lifted and I began my new life as a believer.

God started a great work in me. Soon after, I met my future wife and we got married. I adopted her daughter she had raised by herself and we went on to have three more kids of our own. We were living the normal Christian life. Going to the Baptist church where we got married and involved in the church and related ministry activities. We continued to grow up and moved from our small town to Portland, Oregon.

One day while walking across the street downtown I was suddenly struck by a car that hit me without stopping. I came out of it incredibly bruised and with a lot of back pain. I visited the chiropractor, the physical therapist, and the acupuncturist – none of whom worked. I tried anything I could think of to help relieve my intense back pain.

After over a year, I had heard about kettlebells and how they are helpful in establishing a strong core. Willing to try just about anything, I was immediately sold. I started regularly swinging the kettlebell and after two weeks I was surprised when my back stopped hurting. That was when I began to understand the power of fitness on the human body. There was no stopping at that point.

Soon after, I became a certified personal trainer to help others become stronger the way I had, and for them to have a better version of themselves –beyond their pain. A few years later I became a CrossFit trainer and took my fitness and strength to a whole new level.

I have realized what it takes to become stronger, and the and drive to become a better version of ourselves. didn't realize, however, what it took to become my faith, and why that was important.

years, after first accepting Jesus as my Savior, I ing" Christian, but in my heart I was still God. I knew that I needed to make a change taken a hard hold on my life and I didn't and power of the Holy Spirit to battle it. and minimize the sin on my own –

Through God's grace and mercy, He broke me down and showed me all the areas – marriage, kids, work, etc. – in my life that I was trying to control instead of allowing Him to control them.

I have now begun to learn what it means to commune with the Holy Spirit on a day to day basis, to discover our spiritual gifts, and start activating and exercising those gifts. I've incorporated this lifestyle of living for the Lord everyday and activating our spiritual gifts into my workplace by having an evening of worship, workout, and the Word at my CrossFit gym every month.

God is the author and creator of our lives and He has a specific plan for us. Jesus led the perfect life here on earth; He was God made man. To model our lives after him and follow His example is the way to know God fully. Jesus is our coach, our trainer, and the one who has finished the race well. And we must be imitators of what Jesus did.

Having a personal relationship with the Lord Jesus Christ is similar to developing a training exercise plan. It takes work, stamina, time, and sacrifice. Oftentimes, you have to push through the pain in an effort to allow the Lord to do a great work in your heart so that you come through stronger on the other side.

In reading this book, my hope is that you will desire go beyond the Sunday church routine of life in relationship with God. Simply saying you are a Christi not enough – you need to live a spirit filled life, and tha happens by gaining strength from an effective training p

At the end of each chapter there are a set of discussion questions for you to carefully answer to help you evaluate each chapter's training and specific steps as part of the training plan to help you grow stronger.

Let's get to work!

CHAPTER 1
STRONGER

> *"Be strong in the Lord and in the strength of his might"*
> *Ephesians 6:10*

God wants us to be strong.

Throughout the Scriptures, we are commanded to "be strong." One of the most popular passages used among athletes speaks to the promise of strength: *"I can do all things through Christ who strengthens me"* (Philippians 4:13).

Since strength is defined as our ability to perform a task, it causes us to ask ourselves, "How can we develop the strength necessary to complete the task God has given us?"

Before we answer that question, we must first ask ourselves, "What kind of strength is God calling us to, and how strong does He need us to be? More importantly, why does He want us to be strong?"

In developing fitness, we are accustomed to using the terms strength and power. Physically speaking, we can measure strength and power separately, but the Bible uses these terms interchangeably, since they are both translated from the same original Hebrew expression *chayil*.

We measure strength and power through our performance, or our ability. In the Scriptures, strength is also defined as the "ability to perform," but it is not *our* performance that is measured.

Instead, our strength is found in God's performance. More precisely, our strength is defined by how we measure God's ability.

This book examines the components of a strong faith — **character (virtue), knowledge, self-control, perseverance (steadfastness), godliness, unity (brotherly affection), and love.** Peter, through the guidance and prompting of the Holy Spirit, shared with us how to live a strong, God-focused life in 2 Peter 1:

> ³*His divine power has granted to us all things that pertain to life and godliness, through the knowledge of him who called us to his own glory and excellence,* ⁴*by which he has granted to us his precious and very great promises, so that through them you may become partakers of the divine nature, having escaped from the corruption that is in the world because of sinful desire.*
>
> ⁵*For this very reason, make every effort to supplement your faith with virtue, and virtue with knowledge;* ⁶*and knowledge with, self-control; and self-control with steadfastness, and steadfastness with godliness* ⁷*and godliness with brotherly affection, and brotherly affection with love.* ⁸*For if these are yours and are increasing, they will keep you*

from being ineffective or unfruitful in the knowledge of our Lord Jesus Christ.

⁹For whoever lacks these qualities is so nearsighted that he is blind, having forgotten that he was cleansed from his former sins. ¹⁰Therefore, brothers, be all the more diligent to confirm your calling and election, for if you practice these qualities you will never fall. ¹¹For in this way there will be richly provided for you an entrance into the eternal Kingdom of our Lord and Savior Jesus Christ.

There is no excuse for not living a godly life, for believers have already received everything that is necessary to do so.

After listing these seven values based on a solid foundation of faith in his letter, the Apostle Peter says, *"If these are yours and are increasing, they will keep you from being ineffective or unfruitful in the knowledge of our Lord Jesus Christ"* (2 Peter 1:8).

In other words, as we grow in these qualities, we will stay connected to the One who does the heavy lifting of life and ultimately leads us to the goal of our faith — eternal life.

In the letter to Titus, Paul reminds us that God *"gave Himself for us to redeem us from all lawlessness and purify for himself a people zealous for good works"* (Titus 2:14). Jesus gave His life for a purpose: **to raise up ordinary people who are passionate about advancing the Kingdom of God in this world.**

He provided the perfect model for us to emulate in terms of building His Kingdom. We've heard the phrase: "What you do flows out of who you are." Jesus knew where

He came from, where He was going, and His purpose on this earth. **He served.** What you do—your "works," so to speak—flows out of the person you are. Our actions are an overflow of our inward life. Inevitably, what you do shapes and confirms who you are.

Because we are His, it is important to commit to personal growth to become more Christ-like, and to be more effective in completing His mission. We have been called to be ambassadors, to represent Christ to those living in a fallen world.

Yet, why do we sometimes feel stuck in life? Why are we not growing? Why do we feel like we are walking through life in a haze?

Peter is pretty blunt in verse 9 as he answers with three key words: blindness, shortsightedness, and memory loss. While we are not physically blind, we often find ourselves in a haze, not able to see clearly what God has planned for us. Maybe we are not blind, but rather are shortsighted, only looking at the short-term plan, for today and not the big, eternal picture.

With memory-loss, there are many times that our walk may have led us away from the cross, and the enemy starts up with his mind games, reminding us about our past sins. We forget that Jesus' work on the cross paid for our sins and that if we confess our sins, turn away from the sin, and turn to God with a repentant heart, he will "forgive and forget."

This means that God has forgotten our confessed sins. His work is complete.

Peter is also very clear as to the promise and reward if we possess the qualities that he lists. We will not be idle—or lazy—or spiritually lacking. Our "good works" will be productive. Our focus will be on His Kingdom and the distractions and temptations of the world will not cause us to stumble, for we will know our place and purpose in His plan for us. We are looking toward the "prize", not for gain, but for the wonderful glory of His abundant eternity.

My prayer as you journey through this book is for you to discover and make personal the virtues that Apostle Peter shares with us. These are the key foundations to build a fruitful life that brings you closer to your creator and become the powerful Christian "athlete" He has created you to be.

It all starts with the solid foundation of **Faith**. We have to develop a solid foundation based on faith. This foundation is what everything is built on. It is the DNA of our Christian life. As it is developed deeper, you will become more and more like Him. Upon this solid foundation, we add the other virtues.

We have heard that character is who you are when no one is looking, but character goes deeper than that. **Character** is our thoughts, words, and actions. Our morality, the very essence of who we are, is our character. Sexual sin and our personal agendas defile our heart and create selfishness. No wonder it is the first area that Peter discusses.

Knowledge is more than just head knowledge — it is the experiential knowledge of God and His purposes. We need to know what God wants us to do and then apply ourselves to this spiritual knowledge and understanding. We can sit and read amazing books, like this one, but unless we apply it to our lives, it is useless.

Remember how Paul said asked why we often do the things we don't want to do, and why we don't do the things we should? This is where knowledge and character intersect: **Self-control**. Are there areas in your life that seem out of your control, or are you in bondage to addictions, anger, or lust? What about your physical diet, health, and other aspects of your lives?

Through the work of the Holy Spirit, we must learn how to manage ourselves in this fallen world and continue to endure. Endurance is one of those terms that have a positive and negative connotation associated with them. On one hand, endurance shows that one is able to last a long time in the midst of hardship. On the other, it means that one is in the midst of hardship for a long time. Endurance, or better translated as **Perseverance**, is the ability to maintain a positive attitude during setbacks and pressures. How do you respond in difficulties? When you are squeezed, what comes out of you?

Our respect and reverence toward God has a lot to do with our walk with God. Respect attracts others in a relationship, while disrespect leads to distance in our relationships. Are we cultivating respect in our lives toward Jesus, to His words, His house? To respect someone, we must honor what he or she has to say and who he or she is. Respect, then, should naturally flow toward others in kindness. This is the truest form of **Godliness**.

Our love for others is one of the greatest commandments Jesus taught his disciples. This is true for fellow Christians and those who need to hear His Good News. We need to be **united** in our common cause for His *"will [to] be done on earth as it is in heaven"* (Matthew 6:10).

The ultimate kind of practical kindness is one with no selfish agenda. We are called to "walk in love." **Love** is very practical: it serves people with words and acts of kindness without desire for acknowledgement or recognition.

This is His blueprint for our lives. Just like any athlete who trains, the more an athlete focuses on the fundamentals, the better the athlete gets. As he or she focuses on key aspects of his or her sport, whether it involves coordination, balance, or accuracy, the more tuned he or she is for success.

As you build strength in each of the aforementioned values, God promises an eternal reward and a life full of purpose and wonder. Let's start off our training program by understanding the goals and purpose that God has for us.

DISCUSSION QUESTIONS

1) Name four areas in your personal life where you feel you need to be stronger.

_____

_____

_____

2) What steps of you taken on your own to become stronger in these areas?

_____

_____

_____

3) What have been some areas in your personal life where God's ability and performance were strong?

_____

_____

_____

TRAINING PLAN

As you read through this book, ask yourself the following questions after each chapter, in addition to the training plan items after each chapter:

- What am I doing to strengthen my walk in Christ?

- Which of these qualities do I need to work on?

- What heart issues or bondages block the flow of the Holy Spirit in this area?

- How am I incorporating Jesus' words into my life?

CHAPTER 2
WHAT GOD WANTS

> *"For I know the plans I have for you, declares the Lord, plans for peace and not for evil, to give you a future and a hope."*
> Jeremiah 29:11

Believe it or not, we were not created to be on this earth for a short period of time and live life to accomplish nothing. Be honest. There have been times in your lives where you have asked yourself, "Why am I here? Is this all there is in this life?" There must be something more!

In those questions, however, there is a sign of the problem in our understanding. There is a trend in our culture, a focus on self-idolatry. We are focused on us, on what we want; we are questioning life and our Creator when we wonder if there is more. What makes matters worse is that we are so fueled by our demand for everything instantly — instant coffee, instant communication, instant, gratification, and instant answers.

The unfortunate news is that without addressing our underlying condition, we are left without cause to live for something other than ourselves. We are loyal to only ourselves.

Paul warned Timothy about "us" in 2 Timothy 3:

> *¹But understand this, that in the last days there will come times of difficulty. ²For people will be lovers of self, lovers of money, proud, arrogant, abusive, disobedient to their parents, ungrateful, unholy, ³heartless, unappeasable, slanderous, without self-control, brutal, not loving good, ⁴treacherous, reckless, swollen with conceit, lovers of pleasure rather than lovers of God, ⁵having the appearance of godliness, but denying its power.*

The sad part is found in verse 5, which paints an accurate picture of many of us Christians who are sitting in the church seats on Sunday morning. We have the "appearance of godliness," but we "deny its power."

When we focus on ourselves and on the desires of our hearts, our trying often ends in disaster. The first and biggest error that ultimately led to this heart condition was Eve in the Garden of Eden. Satan spoke directly to the desires of her heart, which led to the fall of Man. Satan and his armies are still at work. In order to separate man from God, Satan lies to us and brings into question our need for God. Satan allows us to believe that we can survive without God and take control of things for ourselves.

In Genesis 16, we can see how well that worked out for Abraham and Sara. Not believing the will of God for their lives, they decided to take matters into their own hands. Their actions caused strife, contempt, and ultimately a speed bump in God's divine plan.

In 1 Samuel 12, the people of Israel repeat their pattern of falling away, entering into bondage, repentance, and return to the Lord. This constant cycle reveals their lack of confidence in their Deliverer. God had provided a way of escape from bondage and offered an environment and Law to help them have a close relationship with Him and to allow them to operate within His Kingdom. However, they demanded for an earthly king, just like all the worldly nations around them.

Far from being an act of repentance, their demand for a king was an act of rebellion. The effect of their sin of *"arrogance…ungratefulness, disobedience, and unholiness"* led the people to "choose" to have a king *"such as all the other nations have."* Sometimes, God will allow hardship and strife to occur in order for us to get us back into His will. Thus, the Lord *"set a king over"* those who conformed to their choice and provided them with Saul. I encourage you to read and discover what kind of king Saul was.

When Josiah refused to listen to God's will, he charged into battle, was shot with a random arrow, and later died from his injuries. The same fate befell Ahab who tried to fool his enemies during battle. Both kings sought after their desires instead of listening and operating within God's will.

Gehazi, the prophet Elisha's servant, took matters into his hands when he thought Elisha had been too lenient on Naaman, who visited them. However, Gehazi focused on the loss of the financial opportunity of the encounter rather than the Kingdom opportunity. Naaman, had shown humility and charity, thankful for the healing he received. Gehazi ended up lying to Naaman and Elisha and suffered physically, and I would imagine eternally as well.

We could continue the numerous examples of humanity rejecting God's plan or operating outside God's will that line the pages of the Bible. Peter finally figured it out later in his life, as he understood God's redemptive grace. But early in his walk with the Lord, he wasn't as mature.

In Matthew 16:22, Peter attempts to inform Jesus that God's plan of ultimately leading Jesus to the cross should be altered. *"Far be it from you Lord! This shall never happen to you."* Peter wasn't listening to Jesus reveal the Kingdom agenda. Peter was focused on the short term. He lacked understanding of the eternal, redemptive plan. The selfish desire to keep his teacher around physically clouded the eternal purpose of what Jesus had just shared with him. No wonder Jesus rebuked Peter so severely. Then Jesus educated Peter to the ultimate weakness, the stumbling block to our ability to get stronger: *"You are not setting your mind on the things of God, but on the things of man"* (Matthew 16:23).

All these examples show that when we try to operate out of selfishness, out of our own desires, we are in conflict with the will of God. We are clouded by our personal desires for fulfillment.

Allow me to use an athlete as an example…Every athlete who has a desire to get stronger has a training program to help them reach his or her goals. An athlete also has the end goal in mind - a roadmap and a destination. He or she also has a trainer to help develop and reach those goals.

God wants us to know His will and His purpose for our lives. Paul exhorts us to not be unwise, but to *"understand what the will of the Lord is"* (Ephesians 5:17). He warns us not to be mindless, or ignorant, or live life recklessly without a plan. Instead, Paul urges us to comprehend fully God's Will. That means we need to have insight, to seek out His will.

No wonder Paul and Timothy prayed for others to be *"filled with the knowledge of his will in all spiritual wisdom and understanding"* (Colossians 1:9). The purpose of this is to *"walk in a manner worthy of the Lord, fully pleasing to him, bearing fruit in every good work and increasing in the knowledge of God"* (Colossians 1:10).

In short, God created us to love Him and to help bring the realities of His Kingdom to this earth. Each of us is a masterpiece, a unique creation of God that He is working on.

Ephesians 2:10 states, *"For we are his workmanship, created in Christ Jesus for good works, which God prepared beforehand, that we should walk in them."* We are in partnership with God when it comes to His will and plan for our lives. His part was to do it all. He bridged the gap that sin had caused through Jesus' sacrifice on the cross. If we believe and rest in the work Jesus did, there is nothing more you can do to become accepted by God.

He designed you for a unique purpose: to advance the Kingdom. We were called to restore our community one life at a time by bringing heaven to earth. The *"works"* that God *"prepared beforehand"* are the activities we do that are driven and energized by the Holy Spirit. God's will is for you to discover your assignment for which He created you to fulfill.

We need to accept the fact that God created us to be **strong**, to regulate our lives, and to become closer to Him so that we can fulfill our assignment. We also need to accept that God *does* have a purpose for us. The author of Psalms recognized this reality when he penned, *"In your book were written, every one of them, the days that were formed for me, when as yet there was none of them"* (Psalm 139:16).

As we get stronger in Him, we develop the ability to walk in His will. The awesome thing is that God wants us to know His will, and He will help us know and discover it. The Bible is the Word of God, and the truths that we need to know in order to live a full life is contained within its pages. However, there are many decisions we need to make in our lives that do not have direct answers in the Bible. Where will I work? Where will I live? Who will I marry?

God helps us know His will through the power of His Holy Spirit. When we put our faith in Jesus and accept His free gift of salvation, we receive the Holy Spirit (Gal. 3:14). God is at work within us, as a power that works within us (Ephesians 3:20) to help us and guide us to will and to do of His good pleasure.

We can only discover God's will and purpose for us if we listen to the Holy Spirit. The Apostle John shares that the Holy Spirit will guide us into all truth. The Holy Spirit is a direct conduit to God, for he *"will not speak on his own authority, but whatever he hears he will speak, and he will declare to you the things that are to come"* (*John 16:13*). One of the main activities of the Holy Spirit is to reveal God's will to us and empower us to do it.

We also, in conjunction with following the Holy Spirit, need to actively pursue our assignment based on what we know. Paul acted upon what He knew, what he concluded as well as upon what the Holy Spirit directed (*Acts 16:6-9*).

One practical way of pursuing our purpose is to look for opportunities to serve and help people. Jesus came to help the whole world, and He left His assignment for the church to carry on the mission. Galatians 6:10 tells us that *"as we have opportunity, let us do good to everyone, and especially to those who are of the household of faith."* Make it a lifestyle of looking for opportunities to help people, and be a blessing to people. That's one way of discovering your assignment because you start to find your way into it quite quickly.

The second way to discover our assignment is to **make a decision to invest in personal growth and development.**

You'll never become great at something unless you get some training. Discover what is inside you that could be a gift to the world, and then develop that gift. Invest in your development. Get some training, get some education, and get some skills. This book is a great start in the right direction.

Develop excellence in serving. Do the little things well, on time, and do it with a grateful heart. Colossians 3:23 says, *"Whatever you do, work heartily, as for the Lord and not for men, knowing"* –here's why you do it this way—*"that from the Lord you will receive the inheritance as your reward."* So serving with excellence is a key part of gaining favor with men, which gives God room to promote you.

Set some practical goals. Make a plan. If you're going to grow and achieve something with your lives, make a plan. Maybe it's just a plan about your work. Whether it's a plan about your spiritual growth, a plan about your marriage, or a plan about your family, you must make a plan. Put some things down that you commit yourself to do. Most people who succeed in life have a plan. They have something that maintains their focus in life.

Build relationships with people who can mentor you or speak into your life. This is one of the things that stop many people from becoming great because they don't actually let anyone speak into their lives, or they don't build connections intentionally with people who can help them grow. If you have an assignment, it requires you to grow, and you need people to help you. So, who do you have speaking into your life? Welcome people to speak into your life to help you grow, then find a place where you can serve.

Take risks; step out and try new things. A good example of this is Peter, who stepped out of the boat on a word from the Lord and began to do something that no man apart from Jesus had ever done before: walk on water. Everyone else played it safe in the boat. Intentionally plan things that stretch you out so you're not comfortable and you have to lean on God. It's in those things where you find your boundaries increase, and you begin to find God moving and making clear what it is that He wants you to do.

We'll never know all that God has for us if we don't try some things out as well as trying different things.

We must pursue our assignment, which is to seek the Kingdom of God first, to make discovering what God has for our lives a priority, and then to accomplish our purpose. Jesus was very aware of His assignment, even at a young age (Luke 2:49). He was totally committed to His assignment (John 4:34), could clearly articulate His assignment (Luke 4:18), and fully completed His assignment (John 17:4).

Jesus didn't just save you to get into heaven. He saved you to fulfill the original purpose, which is to restore the earth, to restore people, and to restore our community, one soul at a time. God wants all of us to be at work, one person at a time, changing our community. It's time to get energized by the Holy Spirit!

Let's follow His training plan as we get Stronger.

DISCUSSION QUESTIONS

1) What are you living your life for?

___

___

___

2) What are some areas that have your time and attention. How many of those are Kingdom focused?

___

___

___

3) How would knowing your purpose contribute to your personal development?

___

___

___

TRAINING PLAN

God wants us to know His will and His purpose for our life. Take some time to seek out His will and journal what the Holy Spirit is saying to you about your purpose. If you do not have your purpose written down, it doesn't exist.

In Matthew 16:22, Peter attempts to inform Jesus that God's plan that leads Jesus ultimately to the cross, should be altered. Peter wasn't listening to Jesus reveal the kingdom agenda. '

"For you are not setting your mind on the things of God, but on the things of man."

Identify areas in your life that you've tried to plan outside of God's plan for you. Pray and hand those areas over to God today.

CHAPTER 3
FAITH

"He grew strong in his faith as he gave glory to God..."
Romans 4:20

Whenever I work with an athlete who wants to get stronger, whether it is in a specific area or just in general, there is always a core set of questions that I ask. I want to find out what I am working with, a starting point if you will. We've all heard the phrase: "You have to start somewhere." This is the beginning point, our foundation.

All of our decisions, thoughts, and actions have brought us to this point. Our upbringing, education, work environment, and family dynamics have formed the foundation of our beliefs, our faith. Just like any foundation of a building, we have a foundation. If the foundation is weak, our building will not be strong.

In Peter's letter, he says, "A*dd to faith*..." Our faith is our foundation. A strong faith creates a strong foundation. A weak faith creates a weak foundation (2 Peter 1:5).

In another letter penned by the Apostle Paul, he helps the believers grow stronger. Paul encourages believers to go on in the purposes of God, but he also says that it is impossible to do this without the strong foundation of faith. The result of this, he shares, is that people remain immature. They remain weak, when God wants us to be strong (Hebrews 6:1-3).

We see this in the lives of Christians. We could be young in our spiritual maturity, even if we have been Christians for quite some time. Maybe we are continually wrestling with failures, shame, guilt, a lack of forgiveness, and tormenting thoughts. Many of us haven't grown in maturity in the power of God to deal with our hearts.

As we mature, we learned how to confront these thoughts with the Word of God. We build a more solid foundation of who we are in God, and we become stronger in His word and through His Spirit. We have become aware of the enemy's tactics and have learned how to subdue them.

The ideal maturity point is to become a spiritual coach. A coach knows the ins and outs of the game, has tremendous experience, and is able to guide others to success. From a spiritual maturity standpoint, the coach knows who God is and is able to reveal God's love to people in such a way that they are attracted to it, and then blessed and benefit from it. Jesus was a spiritual coach to His disciples. He knew and could reveal the love and nature of God to them.

Most young athletes have a role model to whom they look up. Hopefully, their lives are a good example from which they can learn. Unfortunately, we know all too well that even the best role models have flaws. But the concept is still valid. We have people to whom we look up to learn from. No one is perfect except the true role model we should be looking at to get stronger.

Jesus came with a particular mission — He came to reveal what God is like. **He came to reveal the Father and the heart of God as a Father.** In talking with many Christians, both new and mature, they mentioned to me that they have really never known God as a Father. Most of us have formed our foundation of God the Father from our fathers. Some have had good relationships with their father, and some not so good. Some had a father who was very involved in their lives, while the fathers of others were distant and absent. Some were loving, yet some were not. This earthly relationship has formed a foundation of how we view God the Father.

Jesus brought a message that God is a Father, and we can be born again into His family. We can be joined to Him and have His life come into us. We can have a relationship with God as a loving Father. Jesus said to His disciples, "*Whoever has seen me has seen the Father*" (John 14:9).

So, if we want to see what God is like as a Father, we just need to look at Jesus Christ and how He connected with people and how He loved people. In His day, He totally upturned the religious works of the Jewish faith with His love, and Jesus came to invite you and me into a similar relationship.

We're called to turn from dead works and turn instead and replace them with something called Faith toward God. We turn away from activities which are dependent on our own effort and energy, which tire us out, get us drained and frustrated, and make us resentful because we're not getting what we think we should get. A lot of people burn out. Burnouts are often a result of a lot of dead works and wrong motivations; but if we repent of those and we come into Faith in the living God, our lives begin to flourish, and something flows out of it. It's called the life full of the Holy Spirit.

Let's have a look in Hebrews 11:1-3:

"Now faith is the substance of things hoped for, the conviction of things not seen. For by it the people of the old received their commendation By faith we understand that the universe was created by the word of God, so that what is seen was not made out of things that are visible."

Try explaining faith to a kid. They would be asking a bunch of questions trying to figure it out. I bet you are wondering the same thing! What is it? How would I know if I had it? How do I get it? How could I grow and develop it?

These are all important questions. If we desire a strong, solid foundation, and that foundation is built on faith, we need to understand it. The first thing to understand is that faith is different from hope.

Hebrews 11:1 says that faith is the substance of something we hope for. So, hope is about our future, about what is in our minds. It is what we are thinking about, optimistic about, and of which we are expectant—something really good in the future.

Faith is something we have now. Think of it as a conviction and assurance. It's something that we know now, so it is about the present. Hope has to do with the future; faith has to do with the now. Many people confuse faith and hope. They say, "I'm believing God for this," but actually, what they're doing is this: they're hoping that God will do something. Faith is a conviction; it's something we know.

Faith is established in the heart, rather than in the head. *"For with the heart one believes"* (Rom. 10:1). It's amazing that many people—even Christians—can know a lot in the Bible yet have no faith at all. We can know many Scripture verses and still have no faith because it's all in our heads. Faith is an issue of the heart, and with the heart we believe.

All of us believe something. You believe many things about yourself. You believe things about God. You believe things about people. You believe things about life.

Have you ever stopped to evaluate what you really do believe? Many of us have not, and so it's our core beliefs that are what moves us to live the lives we live. It's actually what we believe in our hearts. Those beliefs in our hearts were formed through our experiences, our upbringing, and even our church.

If you had painful experiences when you were younger and felt that you were not of any value, these experiences formed a belief in your heart. If you grew up in a strong, controlling family, in which your opinions or feelings were never considered, you may have formed the angry, resentful, or bitter beliefs that nothing you do is ever good enough, that you'll never get anywhere, or that no one cares about you.

If those beliefs don't change, you will run your life based on those beliefs, which become your belief system. This filters how you go though life. Since faith is established in the heart, what you believe is exactly what you'll have. Since Jesus has shown us the way to the Father and His truth about us, we can look toward Him to shift our beliefs.

God says that you're accepted; but if you don't feel accepted, then you have a struggle in your heart with your belief system.

God says that you're forgiven; but if you don't feel forgiven, then you have a struggle in your heart with your belief system.

God says that you're a child of His and that He's near you all the time; but if you don't feel that He's near you all the time, well, then, you have a struggle in your belief system.

So, we live our lives out of the beliefs we have in our hearts; therefore, it is important for faith to be established in our hearts.

Faith deals with the things that are not seen; nevertheless, the things that are not seen are very real, *"for we walk by faith, not by sight"* (2 Corinthians 5:7). Faith deals with the spiritual realities of God's Word.

The love of God is very real, and when you experience the love of God, it just touches your heart. When you experience God loving you, you feel His presence; so it is real, but not seen. It comes from the realm of the spirit, into the natural realm, by faith.

Everything you and I will receive from God we must have faith in. We must believe what God says about this for it to manifest in our lives.

You may have grown up rejected and believe that you're not acceptable to anyone. Let faith change that, and acceptance will be established in your heart. You are not dependent on what people or circumstances are doing any more.

The Bible says, *"We who have believed enter that rest"* (Hebrews 4:3). So, when faith is present in our hearts, there is also rest from struggle. This struggle is caused when there is conflict between what we see and what God's Word says. Faith should produce a deep confidence that what God says is true in a spiritual sense.

However, we don't want to make light of the struggle. "The struggle is real." Let's say you had a bad day yesterday; there was just so much going on. The kids wouldn't cooperate in the morning. The traffic was bad on the way to work. Someone took your red stapler. You get home expecting a nice, warm, cooked dinner, and instead it's a parental tag team, and it's your turn to deal with those uncooperative kids. So, with that bad day, you forgot to pray, and you now feel distant from God. However, today is a much better day. You wake up refreshed and rested. You have a great quiet time with God, and everything is going your way today. You feel nearer to God or more of Him today.

What changed? God didn't. He was always there. It wasn't really what you did, either. Your 15 minutes of prayer yesterday and two hours today didn't affect how God views you. When you're standing with God—your identity—is secure.

When you receive Jesus Christ as your Savior you become a new person. He puts His Spirit into you. You are now joined to Jesus Christ. You are joined to the Spirit of God. He doesn't break that joining. It is engrafted into you. That's what it means to be "born again". Now, you are not what you used to be; you are a son or daughter of God.

We need to establish this belief, to have faith that we are not who we used to be. The problem is that if we don't accept this truth, we will still live and operate in our old belief system, feeling rejected, afraid, ashamed, broken, and fearful.

You will need to learn the strength of walking with Him. Faith will get you started, and faith will keep you moving forward. It is by grace that God saved you, not by trying hard.

Have you ever noticed that harder you try, the more difficult it gets, and you just want to give up? If you are trying to get right with God in any area of your life by trying to work at it, then you have shifted and come under the Law. Paul said not to frustrate the grace of God. Don't stop God's grace, which is freely and generously given to help you grow and live your life. Don't frustrate it by then trying to perform well to get it.

Don't compete with the grace of God. Stop struggling hard and working to be a better person. Learn to believe what God says is true about you. Allow the Holy Spirit to minister to you and guide you. I've learned that trying to do it on your own without God is impossible.

Jesus said, *"This is the work of God: that you believe"* (John 6:29). The problem is learning to believe. Why? Because immediately, when you believe what God says, the strongholds in your mind and heart rise up and argue; they argue and reason against the will of God. We will explore this more in the next chapter.

It may be hard for you to believe this because of your past experiences, but by building your faith, those past experiences can be transformed.

Paul writes in Romans 4:17 that we must *"call into existence the things that do not exist"*. Faith is expressed through the words we speak. Start speaking words of strength to yourself, and you will notice a change in your belief system. Instead of saying, "I am not worthy," start speaking words of affirmation. Say to yourself, "I am worthy, and I am loved by God." Start speaking God's truth, the Word of God, and you will believe in your heart. When there is faith in your heart, you will confess what God says.

Faith always reaches to what God says in the invisible realm and causes it to manifest now. Sometimes there is a delay between knowing you have it and seeing it happen in life. It requires faith. That is why Jesus taught his disciples to pray, *"Your will be done, on earth as it is in Heaven"* (Matthew 6:10).

But faith is more than just an inward focus. Faith is foundational to our relationship with God. *"For by grace you have been saved through faith. And this is not your own doing; it is the gift of God"* (Ephesians 2:8). Grace is the free gift for which we have to do nothing except believe. That grace is the supernatural, enabling power of God given to us freely. God offered the first step in our relationship with Him, and He provided us with a free gift.

When we accept this gift through faith, Jesus positions us as Children of God—that becomes our new identity. He *"has blessed us with every spiritual blessing in the heavenly places"* (Ephesians 1:3). We have a new nature, identity, acceptance, forgiveness, and redemption. We don't have to work for them because they are ours. That should immediately shift our belief system.

God wants to bless us. Sometimes we look around and say, "Why are they so blessed, and why am I not so blessed?" Well, maybe there's a reason. Maybe they diligently sought God and changed their beliefs. However, it doesn't matter why they are "blessed" and you are not. Each person's blessing is relative to them and their lives. Our responsibility is to have faith in what God will do in our own lives and how He choses to bless us. Faith is foundational to a relationship with God.

Without faith or a trust in God, we can't walk with Him. We can't build any relationship without trust. We can't build a marriage without trust. We can't build a business relationship without trust.

If we argue with God, doubt His truths, try to reason with Him, covet other people's blessings, or try to filter what He says about us through our own opinions, then it is difficult to walk with Him. Walking with God is about developing a relationship of trust with Him, and experiencing His love reinforces this.

Paul instructs us to also *"stand firm therefore, and do not submit again to a yoke of slavery"* (Galatians 5:1-6). We must not fall back into our old ways or our old belief system. We need to learn to receive God's grace and mercy—His Love. It helps to energize our faith.

Just like gaining muscle or getting better at a specific discipline, this requires constant training and exercise. If you want to get better at something, you need to keep working at it. The same is true with our faith. It needs to be flexed and exercised. Our faith can be grown through intimacy and hearing God's voice. Romans 10:17 teaches us, *"Faith comes from hearing, and hearing through the word of Christ."*

Faith is expressed internally in the heart, but the resulting change is expressed on the outside. You may have changed your belief system on the inside, but if there is not a result of an outward change, it really hasn't stuck. A heart change should make a change in the way in which you interact with people, how you think about them, and ultimately, how you serve them.

What about the situations where you have found it difficult to forgive someone who hurt you? Do you find it a struggle to be nice to that person? God's Word says to be nice to that person, yet your heart says to slap their face. You are struggling to be nice, but deep in your heart is hurt and vengeance. You play images through your head about how you would want something bad to happen to them. This isn't the sign of a heart change. You are back to operating in a legalistic, "Law" based belief system, telling yourself, "I have to be nice."

That's why you hear and see so many hypocritical Christians sitting in church. They are finding it really hard to live the Christian life. They have to love people they don't like, including some they may even hate. Other Christian brothers have ripped them off, avoided them, or cut them off. The problem is in their hearts. They are struggling to be good people, but they are not resting in their faith.

God created us to love Him and each other. That is why Jesus says that the two most important commandments are to love Him and love others.

As we begin to meditate on the love God has for us and for others, we will find it coming naturally rather than forced. Build the strength to live a life out of your new identity. Say, "I am a loving person; I love people because that's who I am."

God is good. God loves you, so He wants you to love others. He can love people through you. Faith works by love; so the life of faith is cultivated by spending time with God, beginning to experience His love, and listening to hear His voice, for by hearing His voice, faith suddenly comes into your heart.

Faith grows by meditating in the Word of God and allowing our minds and hearts to be renewed. When faith is there, works flow out that are very real. We don't have to try to love people; love just flows naturally.

When we get filled with the Spirit of God, which is the spirit of love, it flows to touch the world.

When we start to turn to the Lord and allow His Word to shift our hearts, we discover our identity of who He made us to be. That grace and mercy should change our hearts and help us develop and deepen our faith in Him. This heart change begins to repair and transform our belief system, and our faith is made stronger.

We get to see God at work all around us. We get to see His love for others. We get to see His generosity and His forgiveness. And we get to be like Him because we are made in His image.

This is the life of faith. It's a life in which grace and love flow out and touches people. What a great life!

DISCUSSION QUESTIONS

1) Where is your level of faith? (Strong, Neutral, Weak) Try to identify specific areas in which your faith is strong and weak.

2) Have there been there times when you have experienced doubts about God? Discuss the reasons for your doubts, and how you have overcome those.

3) Discuss the ways you have seen God's glory. How have those experiences encouraged you?

TRAINING PLAN

God did not design us to live life with no purpose or plan. We were made have a relationship with God. We were meant to seek Him for the source of our strength. The best way we can accomplish this is through our faith.

With any training program we need to have some daily warmups to accomplish. Each day take time to do the following "exercises":

- Personal study of God's Word
- Fellowship with other believers
- Daily communion with the Holy Spirit that includes open confession of sin & gratitude

Journal the changes along your journey. Its not going to happen overnight. Building strength takes time and sometimes it is difficult to see the change when you look in the mirror each day. By journaling, you are able to look back and see where God was at work in your life, and discover situations that made you stronger.

CHAPTER 4
CHARACTER

> *"We destroy arguments and every lofty opinion raised against the knowledge of God, and take every thought captive to obey Christ"*
> *2 Corinthians 10:5*

The desire to improve is often called the "will to win." It can also be described as striving for excellence. It is the quality athletes possess when they keep training even when conditions look difficult, when no one else is around, and when tangible results cannot be seen.

The Apostle Peter uses a term that is very similar. It can be translated "goodness," "virtue," and "excellence". But, in the athletic arena, it is what has been often called **character**.

So, where does this quality come from? What creates strong character? While faith finds its origins in the heart, character is formed in the mind.

Our **mind** is our moral compass; the decision to do right or wrong is in the mind. The decision to press forward or give up when things get tough is in the mind. Having faith helps, but ultimately, it is our free will—our mind—that determines our action. This is why Peter focuses on this trait as the first floor added to the foundation of faith.

But how does someone train to get stronger in character? What makes one athlete able to endure the mental and physical rigors of training, and another to not? I've been told by one of my mentors that the key to success depends on the space between your two ears.

Outside the athletic arena, many of us do not think to focus on getting stronger in our mind. Too often, we let our thoughts and imagination run wild and rampant.

You might have heard of the book *Battlefield of the Mind* by Joyce Meyer. That title and book could not be more accurate. **What controls our minds will control our lives**, and we are always in a constant battle with it.

In our mind, we are dealing with fear, confusion, self-consciousness, conflict, lust, witchcraft, religious self-importance, assumptions, and pride. The good news is that there is victory in war. In Christ, the battle has already been won (1 Corinthians 15:55–57), but we still need to actively participate in the war. Through Him is victory, but we still must battle. In order to have victory we must engage in the warfare and renew our mind. We need to discipline ourselves to confront the thoughts that are against us and to filter those through the way God sees us. We need to change our patterns of thinking, believing, and responding.

Paul also recognized this battle when he wrote, "*For though we walk in the flesh, we are not waging war according to the flesh. For the weapons of our warfare are not of the flesh but have divine power to destroy strongholds. We destroy arguments and every lofty opinion raised against the knowledge of God, and take every thought captive to obey Christ*" (2 Corinthians 10:3-5).

In any war, it is good to know who your enemy is and who your ally is. The same is true with our thoughts. Not all thoughts are bad. God designed us to be creative, to be able to imagine things not yet existing and bring them into being. Some of these thoughts are placed there by God through the Holy Spirit, some thoughts come from the heart, and others can be evil thoughts or demonic spirits.

In Acts, the disciples received the Holy Spirit during Pentecost. As believers in Christ, we receive the Holy Spirit when we put our faith in Jesus (Acts 8:19). One of the benefits of the Holy Spirit is that "*your sons and daughters shall prophesy, your young men shall see visions, your old men shall dream dreams.*" The Holy Sprit is our conduit to God, and through that conduit, God can place within us prophetic thoughts, pictures, and images. These images are promptings from God to unlock potentials, possibilities, and destinies.

As mentioned before, God loves us and wants us to fulfill our purpose and destiny. Even as God provided simple, basic needs to His people, such as food and water (Nehemiah 9:15), he also provides clues and direction for us. Our mind should be open and yielded to the Holy Spirit-inspired pictures and possibilities.

The prophet Jeremiah stated, "*I know the plans I have for*

you, declares the Lord, plans for welfare and not for evil, to give you a future and a hope" (Jeremiah 29:11). God gave Jeremiah hope, something for him to look forward to, and God wants you to have hope and direction as well.

Break out of your current thinking about God, Jesus, and the Holy Spirit. Do not be confined to the ways of the world or religious practice. Be willing to open yourself to the promptings of the Holy Spirit. Are we recognizing His voice through our thoughts?

Another form of our thoughts can be from bondage by demonic spirits. I'm not talking about being possessed here, but throughout Scripture, we see Satan and his army using thoughts to attack those who are pursuing a relationship with God.

It started in the garden. Satan brought into question God's Word. The devil put a seed of doubt, a thought that opposed God. That's the easiest way to determine if the thought is from God or not. If it is in opposition to God, His plan, and His world, it's safe to say that it is from the devil. Satan tried it again with Jesus' temptation in the desert. The first thing Satan used to try to break Jesus was to get him to question His identity with God. Satan said to Him, "***IF** you are the son of God…*" (Luke 4:3). Satan will bring up past sins and thoughts, and then accuse us of not being saved or transformed. He tries to plant in our thoughts images that invade and fill our mind with feelings and pictures that oppose God.

We then take those thoughts, ponder them, enter into them, and conceive the sin. Just like Eve did in the Garden, she looked at the fruit, took it, ate it, and then gave it to someone else. Sin is always first conceived in our thoughts. We ponder it, wonder if it's going to be okay. We start to question if we can get away with it. We justify it. The mind is where strongholds of bondage to fear, anxiety, lust, gossip, and pride exist. When our minds become corrupt, we cannot see God's vision clearly anymore. *"No longer walk as the Gentiles do, in the futility of their minds"* (Ephesians 4:17).

As mentioned in the last chapter, the heart is the keeper of faith. Proverbs says to *"keep your heart with all vigilance for from it flow the springs of life"* (Proverbs 4:23). What you truly believe in your heart will show. So, **the heart and mind are connected.** Mark agreed when he stated, *"For from within, out of the heart of man, come evil thoughts"* (Mark 7:21).

Some thoughts arise from our heart. These could be dreams, desires, possibilities, or aspirations. But thoughts also arise from areas out of our own life that need cleansing.

The dreams of our hearts have been placed there by God —written by Him. *"For it is God who works in you, both to will and to work for to His good pleasure"* (Philippians 2:13). They are there to please God. He wants to see you flourish, prosper, and have a fruitful life. Dream big dreams, and turn them into practical steps utilizing the gifts He provided to empower you through the Holy Spirit.

However, many of us have stopped dreaming. We have memories of past hurts, wounds, and painful experiences. We have undisciplined thoughts in regards to fear, anxiety, and rejection. We often escape into a comfortable place in our thoughts and become desensitized to the evil in this world.

I imagine you have heard the proverb, *"As he thinks in his heart, so is he"* (Prov. 23:7). The biggest issue we face in our minds is probably the easiest to reverse: ungodly beliefs, attitudes, and expectations that we have developed through life. Ungodly beliefs are statements we claim and hold to be true that are in direct opposition to who God is and who He created us to be.

For example, you've probably thought some of these statements a few times in your life:

- I don't belong.
- I will never have any money.
- No one cares how I feel.
- The best way to avoid being hurt is to isolate myself.
- I am too fat.
- I am unattractive.
- I am the problem; something is wrong with me.
- I am bad; if people knew me they would reject me.
- I should have been a boy/girl.
- I need to plan everything.
- It must be my fault.
- I must guard my feelings.
- If I let anyone close, they will hurt me.
- I should never trust anyone in authority over me.
- God loves others more than He loves me.
- No matter what I do, it is not good enough.

If you have a mind that has run away from you, you need to come back, confront your thoughts, speak the Word of God to yourself, and discipline your mind. It must be a daily battle.

When your heart and mind are not renewed, you will stay in the wrong beliefs, have incorrect conclusions and wrong assumptions, and ultimately, blame others or God. As a Christian, if you do not deal with this pattern of incorrect thinking, the pattern will repeat itself and condemnation will follow. This is why you may not feel like you are moving ahead. The war is waged in the battlefield of our mind.

"For though we walk in the flesh, we are not waging war according to the flesh. ⁴For the weapons of our warfare are not of the flesh but have divine power to destroy strongholds. ⁵We destroy arguments and every lofty opinion raised against the knowledge of God, and take every thought captive to obey Christ, ⁶being ready to punish every disobedience, when your obedience is complete" (2 Corinthians 10:3-6).

We are not able to serve God effectively until we know how to capture and conquer our thoughts. I want to give you some basics to apply to your life right now, to help you get stronger in your character.

Paul instructs the believers in Corinth that this battle is not a physical battle, but a spiritual one, a battle that is won by the Word of God. Your thoughts are subject to the Word of God. This is your spiritual weapon: God's truth found in the pages of your Bible that is collecting dust on your nightstand.

Another way to read 2 Corinthians 10:3-6 is "the weapons of our warfare are not carnal, but mighty through God." Only through God and His Word and His power through the Holy Spirit can we obtain victory. Paul uses the word "destroy," or "pull down." Think of a large crane or wrecking ball that is pulling down a large brick wall with force. Strongholds are not puny little walls. Satan and his army have taken control of our minds for far too long.

God's Word has instructed us to "take every thought captive." This means to lead away, to capture, and to bring under control. We are to exercise dominion over and subdue ungodly thoughts. We need to shut them down and stop them from ruining our minds. Paul reminded the Roman believers to *"not be conformed to this world, but be transformed by the renewal of your mind"* (Romans 12:2). We need to transform our thoughts to what God says about our lives, not the lies that the enemy says. Transformation is a total change.

The good news is that we **can win** this war. We need to learn how to fight back. We need to be able to recognize the thought and take it captive. Don't be defeated with the thought. It happens to everyone: memories, imagination, pictures. We need to respond immediately and confront it. Don't feel condemned; stand up against it.

We also need to speak and declare God's truth, His Word. The sword of the Spirit is the Word of God. When a negative or ungodly thought enters in, we need to declare what God says. Speak to the thought, use the authority given to us by Christ, take dominion over the thought, and cancel its operation.

Are thoughts of worry consuming your mind and time? Are you trying to figure it all out? Turn to 1 Peter 5:7 and cast *"all your anxieties on him, because he cares for you."*

With all these Scriptures available to you, take the time to memorize and meditate on them. Picture the truth of the

Scripture and hold it in your thoughts. Embrace what you see; let those thoughts be the ones that transform your mind. Make it more than just about Scripture memorization. Imagine the feeling associated with the Scripture. Picture Jesus standing next to you as you make those declarations. Imagine standing in the throne room having a conversation with God and hearing Him speaking His truth over you. See His powerful words tearing down those strong holds.

Make it a habit to repeat those verses on a daily basis. Repetition not only writes it upon your mind, but also upon your heart. This process will establish new patterns of thinking and help renew your mind. James 1:21 tells us to *"receive with meekness the engrafted word which is able to save your souls."* The term "Engrafted" means to join something into an existing root. We are to take the written Word of God and graft it into our ways of thinking. Implant it so it takes root and grows.

Repeat God's truth both in your mind and out loud. Jesus said, "It is the Spirit who gives life; the flesh is no help at all. The words that I have spoken to you are spirit and life." Speaking the Word of God activates the Holy Spirit and life into us. Personalize and speak Scripture over your life repeatedly. Saturate your mind, emotions, and thoughts with the Word of God until truth takes root and produces fruit. This will take some strength, as we need to develop our mental muscles. However, the more we work on them, the stronger they will get.

In Psalms, we see that healing takes place through His Spirit and His Word.

"He restores my soul. He leads me in paths of righteousness for his name's sake." Psalm 23:3

"The Law of the LORD is perfect, reviving the soul; the testimony of the LORD is sure, making wise the simple." Psalm 19:7

Jesus told His disciples that when the Holy Spirit comes —the Spirit of Truth—He would guide them into all truth, the truth of God's Word. The Holy Spirit will also lead you on the right path. He will accompany you on your journey to healing. His truth will take you where you need to go. The Holy Spirit can reveal Jesus to you, and what you see and hear will begin to overwrite your old memories. Take a look at the full picture from a spiritual perspective, and ask the Holy Spirit for discernment to see God's Hand in the situation.

Finally, refocus and direct your thoughts somewhere else. Matthew 6:22 shares wise words from his teacher, *"The eye is the lamp of the body. If your eyes are good, your whole body will be full of light."* Don't be dragged away by temptation and vain imaginations. Tear these thoughts down, speak the Word of God into them, and break through self-pity, poverty, fear, and inferiority.

Say to yourself, "Don't be afraid of what's in this world. You are not of this world. The Father has sent you to make a difference in this world."

Stay strong in your thoughts. Allow what happens in your mind to become a reflection of who God is and how He sees you.

DISCUSSION QUESTIONS

1) Why is character important?

2) How do your thoughts about yourself influence your character?

3) What kind of character does God want us to have? Be specific.

TRAINING PLAN

Review your previous discussion questions answers and evaluate how your thoughts affect your character. Remind yourself of what God says about you.

*"For I know the **plans** I have for you, declares the Lord, **plans** for welfare and not for evil, to give you a future and a hope"* (Jer. 29:11).

CHAPTER 5
KNOWLEDGE

> *"For flesh and blood has not revealed this to you,*
> *but my Father who is in heaven"*
> Matthew 16:17

What are the most common excuses given for not participating in an intense exercise training program? Often, we hear this one: "I am not ready to start training with that kind of intensity until I get in better shape. I will train on my own until I get in better condition, and then I will join the class." Those who are experienced in exercise training know that this is the worst thing a person can do. The best way for an athlete to prepare for functional movements at high intensity is to practice these same movements with a knowledgeable coach who can **scale** to the athlete's current ability. The best way to get better and stronger at a movement is to do it. The same is true with our spirituality.

However, we are following a disturbing trend. More and more evangelical Christians do not seem to be holding true some of the most basic theological concepts in the Bible. Why? That could be a long topic, but I would sum it up by explaining that Christians are not taking Peter's teaching seriously. They are not growing stronger in their experiential knowledge of God and His purposes. Many have come to Christ, attend church on Sunday, and maybe go to a small group, but outside of these situations, they are not fully experiencing God at a deep spiritual level.

We all have trouble with it; we all have other parts of our lives that seem to get in the way. Or maybe we just see growing closer to God as work, and we do not take joy in it any longer because we feel that our efforts have failed. Some may say, "Yeah, but I am saved, isn't that enough?"

We are not called only to salvation; we are called to serve God, to grow in His image, and to share His truth. We are called to grow in the knowledge of Him and to live life to the fullest with God for His glory.

How does knowledge help us grow stronger in our faith? In Acts 8:26-40, we read of an Ethiopian eunuch who was pursuing a relationship with God on his own. He was not lacking in self-discipline or desire, but his knowledge was incomplete. After traveling many miles to worship, he was reading the Scriptures on his own. He encountered truth that he could not grasp without the help of a teacher.

With great humility, he accepted the invitation to hear the truth through an evangelist named Philip. Upon hearing this new truth, he quickly decided to obey the Lord. This began his journey of walking with the Lord. Specifically, what knowledge did the Ethiopian encounter? *"Then Philip opened his mouth, and beginning with this Scripture he told him the good news about Jesus."*

The result was life changing for the Ethiopian. He received a revelation, a shift in his thinking. It was more than just knowledge; it was a spiritual experience.

God impacts lives through revelation.

Matthew 16:17-19 states, *"And Jesus answered him, 'Blessed are you, Simon Bar-Jonah! For flesh and blood has not revealed this to you, but my Father who is in heaven. And I tell you, you are Peter, and on this rock I will build my church, and the gates of hell shall not prevail against it. I will give you the keys of the Kingdom of heaven, and whatever you bind on earth shall be bound in heaven, and whatever you loose on earth shall be loosed in heaven.'"*

Peter received revelation of who Jesus Christ is—not from his own knowledge, but from the knowledge that was God-given, inspired by the Holy Spirit. The foundation of the church was built upon that revelation.

Jesus also taught, *"Whoever hears these words of mine and does them, I will liken him to a wise man who builds his house upon a rock."* Hearing God's revelation of knowledge and responding by faith and action forms a solid foundation.

But **receiving a revelation may challenge your mindset and beliefs**. In Acts 10:9-16, Peter had a vision and received revelation of how big God is and how big God's love is for all people. However, Peter's first reaction was from his old beliefs and traditions. "I have never eaten anything common or unclean" is a statement locked into Jewish tradition and the Law in which Peter was raised. Even upon seeing what Jesus had done, Peter's concept of God was small and limited in his mind to the Jewish nation. He initially resisted the greatness of God's grace, which included non-Jews. God's love was for all people, and this was hard for Peter to grasp.

Sometimes, God's revelation will have an impact on our thinking. It may even challenge our beliefs and faith. We may resist these revelations due to wrong emotional perceptions of God and people. Or, we may have wrong or inadequate foundations that are steeped in traditions. We might be resisting His revelation based upon pressure to conform to group beliefs. Worst of all, we might refuse to admit that we are wrong, as pride overcomes hearing God's voice.

Peter had an experience of God that challenged the wrong beliefs from which he had operated with a mindset of the Law. He was a follower of Jesus, received the baptism of the Holy Spirit, and had led numerous people to the knowledge and revelation of their Messiah. However, God had a bigger purpose for Peter, and it led to spreading the Gospel to all nations, all races, and all languages, for all His people.

Still not convinced that you need to receive a stronger revelation from the Lord? Do you have it all figured out? Still sitting in the pews, but not fully experiencing what God has planned for you? Still not operating in the fullness of God's character and power? Let's see how a life can be altered completely through gaining a revelation of who God is and the power that He promised us.

I imagine you have heard about the transformation of Saul to Paul in Acts 9. Go check it out if you haven't read it. Please do that now, and see if that helps.

Paul gives a bit of a back-story of who he was before he received his revelation. In Philippians 3:5-6, Paul gives us a snapshot of his foundational beliefs, traditions, and actions. He was a devout Jew, a person of the nation of Israel, a descent of Jacob, from the tribe of Benjamin. He was born and raised by Hebrew parents who followed the Law, and therefore he was circumcised on the eighth day. His educational background was based the Law taught by the Pharisees. He was actively committed to his religion as his concern for the Law was blameless, and he was zealous for God. His life was built solidly on the foundation of the Law, and he was convinced that it was the only way to live. He was so passionate about people who broke the Law as to punish them by death if they were against the Law. In his mind, he was fully committed to God, yet the foundation of his belief system was inadequate for the New Covenant that Jesus created. This left his life to be filled with lack of fruitfulness, resentment, and frustration, which led to a controlling behavior, persecution of innocent believers, and even murder, which was against the Law.

When God provides a revelation, He is not trying to conform us and force us into something different. He is doing it out of grace and mercy. There are consequences to living a life that is based on incorrect beliefs and Laws.

Paul was acting out his beliefs, "breaking threats and murder." His consequences of living a life based on the Law was exposed by a simple question from God: *"Saul, Saul why are you persecuting me?"* In one moment, Saul received a revelation from God.

God wasn't angry. He didn't threaten Paul or come out with direct accusations. He did however treat him with honor and grace. All God did was ask a simple question. He does that to invite us to examine our inner beliefs, to challenge us. God revealed who He was through Jesus.

Sometimes when we receive revelation, it may not be the full, complete picture. After revealing who Jesus was and what Paul was doing to Him by killing his people, God gave Paul a simple assignment. Not the entire plan, just the next step.

When we receive revelation, it may just be the beginning piece to start us on our journey. We may not know what the end result is. In many cases, revelation is progressive. We must walk it out in faith and yield ourselves to the teaching, training, and ministry that may come with it. We also must humble ourselves to receive the revelation. This may mean prayer and fasting to prepare to receive more of what God has for us.

Once the work had begun through God's grace, Paul applied himself to study and understand the significance of the change. He came to know that it was only through God's grace that he became the leader of the early church. He then helped others realize and grow stronger in their beliefs and helped lead them deeper in their knowledge of God. Paul guided them in their spiritual experience to gain more knowledge of God.

What are some of the foundational beliefs and legalistic views you have right now that God is graciously asking you to let go of? Are you at a point in your Christian journey where it seems like you are stuck?

Ask God for a revelation, knowledge, wisdom, or a spiritual experience that will change your paradigm.

Ask God for a deeper understanding of the Bible, who Jesus is in your life, the Holy Spirit, His Hand at work daily, living a life full of the Spirit with the character of God and His power flowing abundantly.

The good news of Christ is not merely "book knowledge." Just like our training, it can only be acquired through experience. The Greek term for "knowledge" in the New Testament emphasizes that which is gained through a firsthand relationship.

As disciples of Christ, we do not have a relationship with a manual. More rules or information will never be enough to connect us to God. We can only find grace and peace through a deeper knowledge of Jesus Christ gained by a firsthand relationship with Him through the Holy Spirit. Listen to Him every day through studying His Word. Speak to Him in prayer by sharing your desires, hopes, and fears. Allow your relationship with Him to develop through fellowship with the One whom He gave us to build that relationship. The good news is that Jesus gave us an understanding and a way to know Him and His Father in John 14.

"⁷If you really know me, you will know my Father as well. From now on, you do know him and have seen him." ⁸Philip said, "Lord, show us the Father and that will be enough for us."

> ⁹*Jesus answered: "Don't you know me, Philip, even after I have been among you such a long time? Anyone who has seen me has seen the Father. How can you say, 'Show us the Father'? ¹⁰Don't you believe that I am in the Father, and that the Father is in me? The words I say to you I do not speak on my own authority. Rather, it is the Father, living in me, who is doing his work."*

How does the Father live in Jesus? Through the Holy Spirit. Remember Jesus' baptism and the Spirit of the Lord coming to rest upon Jesus like a dove?

> ¹¹*Believe me when I say that I am in the Father and the Father is in me; or at least believe on the evidence of the works themselves. ¹²Very truly I tell you, whoever believes in me will do the works I have been doing, and they will do even greater things than these, because I am going to the Father. ¹³And I will do whatever you ask in my name, so that the Father may be glorified in the Son. ¹⁴You may ask me for anything in my name, and I will do it.*

Jesus gives us the way to the most powerful knowledge anyone can acquire. Jesus teaches us how to understand what a relationship with Him looks like and how we are to walk out that relationship. Jesus says that whoever believes in Him will do what He has been doing and even more. What has Jesus been doing and what does he want us to do?

> ¹⁵*"If you love me, keep my commands. ¹⁶And I will ask the Father, and he will give you another advocate to help you and be with you forever— ¹⁷the Spirit of truth. The world cannot accept him, because it neither sees him nor knows him. But you know him, for he lives with you and will be in you. ¹⁸I will not leave you as orphans; I will come to you. ¹⁹Before long, the world will not see me anymore, but you will see me. Because I live, you also will live. ²⁰On that day you will realize that I am in my Father, and you are in me, and I am in you. ²¹Whoever has my commands and keeps them is the one who*

loves me. The one who loves me will be loved by my Father, and I too will love them and show myself to them."

Here is some foreshadowing of what we are supposed to do with that knowledge:

²²Then Judas (not Judas Iscariot) said, "But, Lord, why do you intend to show yourself to us and not to the world?" ²³Jesus replied, "Anyone who loves me will obey my teaching. My Father will love them, and we will come to them and make our home with them. ²⁴Anyone who does not love me will not obey my teaching. These words you hear are not my own; they belong to the Father who sent me. ²⁵"All this I have spoken while still with you. ²⁶But the Advocate, the Holy Spirit, whom the Father will send in my name, will teach you all things and will remind you of everything I have said to you."

Jesus clearly states that if we love Him, then we will obey Him. We need to experience the fullness of His love for us. This love comes through the Holy Spirit into our lives.

The message of Christ is the most vital knowledge anyone can gain. All other teaching, experiences, and practices must be understood in light of this knowledge. Through this knowledge, we are promised the power of grace, peace, and all things necessary for life and godliness.

DISCUSSION QUESTIONS

1) What do you know about God? What are some specific areas of knowledge you have of God?

2) Why is it important to know who God is?

3) How does knowledge help us grow stronger in our faith?

TRAINING PLAN

Knowing Christ is not merely "book knowledge." Just as you cannot read a book and immediately become better at a skill or a movement, the same is true with our walk with Christ.

We cannot just read the Bible and say that we know him more. Our knowledge of Jesus Christ is only made deeper with an experiential relationship with him. Only here can we find grace and peace.

Listen to Him every day through studying His Word. Journal passages that stand out to you.

Speak to Him through prayer by sharing your desires, hopes, and fears. Be silent and listen to the Holy Spirit.

Allow your relationship with Him to develop through fellowship with the body of Christ - His church.

CHAPTER 6
SELF-CONTROL

> *"Keep your heart with all diligence for out of it are the issues of life."*
> Proverbs 4:23

What ultimately makes an athlete successful?

When natural ability and opportunities are not enough to help us excel, we are forced to find additional tools to help us continue our pursuit of excellence in our particular sport. No matter how talented we may be, we all come to a point where we must commit to training if we are going to continue improving in our sport.

> *"If you put these things before the brothers, you will be a good servant of Christ Jesus, being trained in the words of the faith and of the good doctrine that you have followed. 7 Have nothing to do with irreverent, silly myths. Rather train yourself for godliness; 8 for while bodily training is of some value, godliness is of value in every*

way, as it holds promise for the present life and also for the life to come. 9 The saying is trustworthy and deserving of full acceptance. 10 For to this end we toil and strive, because we have our hope set on the living God, who is the Savior of all people, especially of those who believe" (1 Timothy 4:6-10)

God's Word instructs us to "train for godliness." The word for "train" in the Bible means to vigorously exercise like an Olympic athlete with resistance and discipline. It includes total commitment and the will to remove all distractions that can keep us from pursuing our goal.

Paul taught Timothy that the greatest distraction from training is the act of placing our focus on ourselves rather than the source of our power. We must be *"trained in the words of the faith."* When we taste success, it can be tempting to stop relying on what got us there. And, similarly, when we experience defeat, it is common for us to stop listening to coaching. However, a successful athlete stays focused on the goal no matter the results and never forgets the true source of his or her power.

Paul urged Timothy to concentrate his energy on vigorous training for genuine godliness. For Paul, genuine godliness involved both right belief and obedient action. Godly habits do not appear without determined human purpose and effort. Timothy was to persist in that Christian discipline, which eventually prepared him for God's highest purposes.

And that is God's desire, that each one of us to grow stronger in our maturity (Heb. 6:1-2).

Maturity is connected to our personal responsibility and our perspective of our experiences. Personal responsibility involves embracing ownership of what God has entrusted to us. Are you a good steward of your choices, emotions, resources, and relationships? It is also about taking responsibility for of what we have been entrusted to do, and for the consequences of not doing what we were supposed to do.

Perspective is how you view what you see, especially from your experiences. How you view your world determines your feelings and actions. **When we have a worldly perspective, we focus on ourselves. When we have a Godly perspective, then we focus on God.** The main reason for the Fall was the loss of God's perspective in exchange for personal gain. Adam and Eve failed to value their relationship with God and forgot to honor the source of their blessing.

The choices you make determine the course of your life. The decisions you make on a day-to-day basis have long lasting effects. God's greatest gift to each of us is the gift of free will. He gave us the ability to make decisions. Most of those decisions can seem small or unimportant, but they do accumulate. Over a long period of time, the results of choices can be easily seen.

Think about it this way. All your best decisions have gotten you to the point where you are today, including decisions regarding finances, family, health, education, and spiritual growth. Your choices have an impact on you and on the next generation.

As I mentioned before, your heart has a big influence on your decisions. Proverbs 4:23 states to *"keep your heart with all diligence for out of it are the issues of life."* We view life through the filters we have in our hearts.

Our mindset often has influence on our decisions. Peter's mindset in Acts 10:14 was that he had never eaten an unclean animal, yet in his vision, He was directed to do so. This ultimately led to Peter preaching the Gospel to Gentiles.

In Matthew 7:1-5 we learn about the danger of judging others when we ourselves deserved to be judged. We cannot see clearly because of our short sightedness about a situation. We make assumptions and accusations about someone or something without all the information.

Even Jesus ran into opposition in his own town as He tried to share about God's Kingdom through signs and wonders. Many people took offense of His teachings because they knew Him as a boy growing up, running around the streets of his hometown. Offenses often create a negative filter that makes it difficult to see the situation clearly.

Here is the truth about how God created us: He created us for a relationship—with Him, and with others. We have no choice whether to participate or not, only how to participate. God also gave us the capacity to choose how we relate with each other and the motivation. Are you focused on helping others or hindering them? Are you focused on others or just yourself? God also created you with the ability to take responsibility for yourself. You can choose your thoughts, your feelings, your beliefs, and your actions. You decide how you think and react. You are responsible for your choices.

Romans 14:10-13 states that, *"each of us shall give account of himself before God."*

Remember when as a child you did something you were not supposed to, and when asked by your parents who did it, you refused to take responsibility for your actions? This reminds me of the Family Circle comics depicting the "Not me", "I dunno", and "Nobody" characters when the parents ask their kids a question that they do not want to own up to. 1 Corinthians 13:11 states that, *"when I became a man I put away childish things."*

When it comes down to it, self-control is all about the moment of decision. That one point when you choose the road to take. As mentioned before, our thoughts, feelings, and beliefs have a direct correlation to our actions. This may result in either positive or negative consequences.

Since God gave us the ability to choose, let's honor Him and take responsibility for our own feelings, thoughts, expectations, assumptions, and judgment. His word says that, *"each one shall bear his own load"* (Galatians 6:5). We need to believe that everything that happens can be changed with God's truth, for *"all things work together for good to those who love God, to those who are called according to His purpose."*

When we find ourselves lacking the power to achieve our goals, that is when it comes time to evaluate our training. Are we training enough? Have we forgotten why we train? Have we lost the motivation to train due to success? Or, have we lost our motivation due to failure?

Jesus reminds His disciples that a lack of training is a lack of faith. **When we stop praying, we have stopped believing in the power of God.** And, when we stop believing in God's power, we are attempting to take over. In order to "train for godliness," we must keep our goal in front of us at all times. This will focus our attention on the only One who can get us to God. He is our motivation and the reason we keep training.

"This is why we work hard and continue to struggle, for our hope is in the living God, who is the Savior of all people and particularly of all believers" (1 Timothy 4:10).

DISCUSSION QUESTIONS

1) What areas of your life do you think need more self-control?

2) Does your level of faith in God affect your lack of/or need for self-control?

3) Evaluate what areas of your life influence you more than God's Word or instruction for how you should live.

TRAINING PLAN

When we find ourselves lacking the strength to achieve our goals, it's time to evaluate our training. Are we training enough? Have we forgotten why we train? Have we lost the motivation to train due to success? Or, have we lost our motivation due to failure?

Jesus reminds his disciples a lack of training is a lack of faith. When we stop praying, we have stopped believing in the power of God. And, when we stop believing in God's strength we are attempting to take over.

We must keep our goal in front of us at all times – to become more like Christ. He is our motivation and the reason we keep training.

Journal your walk with Christ journey up to this point. Identify key milestones where you felt strong and where you were weak.

CHAPTER 7
PERSEVERANCE

> *"We rejoice in our sufferings, knowing that suffering produces endurance" (Romans 5:3)*

Vince Lombardi famously said, "Fatigue makes cowards of us all." The main quality athletes must develop in order to prevent fatigue's effect is **endurance**. Without endurance, an athlete cannot be successful. But how is it developed? The Scriptures say that there is only one way, and that is through suffering. *"We rejoice in our sufferings, knowing that suffering produces endurance."*

1 Corinthians 10:13 reads, *"No temptation has overtaken you except such as is common to man, but God is faithful, who will not allow you to be tempted beyond what you able, but with the temptation will also make the way of escape that you may be able to bear it."*

Temptation means to put something to proof or to a test. Every person faces pressures and difficulties in life; storms can come unexpectedly. These storms can take on difference forms, including financial, physical health, marriage, family, relationships, work, and ministry.

But in 1 Corinthians 10:13, we learn that there is a *"but God"* statement. I love but God statements. These mean that despite what we are facing, God is always there. He promises:

- You are not the only one facing this.
- He is faithful. He will never leave you and will always help you.
- You are up to the challenge even if you think you are not.
- He has a way for us to walk through the storm and grow.

So, how do we confront our storms? Let's look at Mark 4:35-41, which discusses storms and how to deal with them.

^{35}On that day, when evening had come, he said to them, "Let us go across to the other side." ^{36}And leaving the crowd, they took him with them in the boat, just as he was. And other boats were with him. ^{37}And a great windstorm arose, and the waves were breaking into the boat, so that the boat was already filling. ^{38}But he was in the stern, asleep on the cushion. And they woke him and said to him, "Teacher, do you not care that we are perishing?" ^{39}And he awoke and rebuked the wind and said to the sea, "Peace! Be still!" And the wind ceased, and there was a great calm. ^{40}He said to them, "Why

are you so afraid? Have you still no faith?" ⁴¹*And they were filled with great fear and said to one another, "Who then is this, that even the wind and the sea obey him?"*

Jesus and His disciples were on a mission. Jesus' purpose and priority is clear: to seek and save lost people. God always wants to reach people with the Gospel, and oftentimes that means stepping outside of your comfort zone and crossing over to the other side to expand the Kingdom. If we sometimes feel stuck in life, it's probably because we've stopped moving. Jesus' mandate was to the harvest. Everything He did had a direction and a purpose.

Have we lost our direction? Our purpose in life? Do we have a plan for the coming year? Do we know why God has put us on this earth? Are we walking out the plan He has for us in faith?

Jesus had in mind a territory to be reached. He had a vision of a whole region of people He wanted to reach with the Gospel. So, when Jesus said told His disciples to move to a new place, He wanted to move forward, not to stay with the comfortable or with those who had already heard Him. He wanted to move forward.

God is speaking to us about the need for us to break out of our limitations, to break out of our comfort zones. Have we become comfortable with mediocrity? Have we become comfortable with our surroundings and those around us who keep us from moving forward? Jesus *"left the multitude,"* the comfort of the crowd, to pursue His Father's priority. To move forward and break through, **we need to do the**

uncomfortable until it becomes comfortable.

However, many times, when we attempt to move forward, that's when things always seem to go wrong. We have to just understand the reality that when we move forward, there are two warring clashes that take place: the Kingdom of God and the kingdom of darkness. A lot of Christians are not aware that, as we move forward in God's destiny for our lives, there is a spiritual conflict. It requires that we overcome some of the things that rise against us. It always costs us something when we focus on the harvest.

According to the words that were used to describe the "great storm," a storm includes black thunderclouds, strong gusts of wind, and torrents of rain. Great means mega—very big. This wasn't a little wind and rain. It was a very big storm with strong gusts of wind, torrents of rain, and pretty much hurricane or gale force winds that tossed the boat around. It kind of reminds me of some of the storms of life I have been in, when everything felt so stormy and was coming against me, and I felt like I was sinking in life.

To understand how to endure these storms, it's good to learn why we are in storms in the first place. There are **four different types of storms**:

The first storm is the **storm of your own making**. This is a storm that you have brought upon yourself.

A storm of our own making is caused by stuff we did, or didn't do but should have, and then suffer its consequences. For example, if you spend more money than you have coming in, a financial storm is about to arise. It's only a matter of time before it arises. What's our typical reaction? You complain that the devil is attacking you or that God is not coming through. The reality is that you goofed up! It's just as simple as that. You mismanaged your finances, and now you're reaping what you sowed.

Now the problem with this is that we don't always see the connection between our actions and the current storm. Sometimes, a bit of time passes before you finally start to reap the consequences of your actions and your inner storm, whether it be in your marriage, your family, your finances, your personal life, or your work life.

The self-imposed storm is the result of neglect, or poor choices. This is not a storm in which you just pray about it and blame the devil on it. You have to own it and take full responsibility. You will only have power over the storm when you own up to responsibility. One of my pastors always said, "Choose to sin, choose to suffer."

The second kind of storm is a **God-directed storm**. In this storm you can't work your way out, pray your way out, or repent your way out. God is the one who blew in the thing in the first place to bring about a change, a place of surrender and alignment.

Just look at the classic example of Jonah. He had been told by the Lord to go and preach the Gospel in Nineveh. He didn't want to go, he didn't like the land, so he went out of his way to steer clear of the destiny that God had placed on his life. Therefore, God sent a storm.

And the bad part is that everyone around you gets caught

up in your storm. You may be married but going in the wrong direction, so the whole family is in turmoil because you are not doing what God says.

God lets some storms happen for a purpose. Its purpose is to realign us with the Kingdom so we don't go off track any further. Are you going exactly 180 degrees away from where God wants you to go? The reason you might be in this storm is because you are not in a right place in your heart.

God is helping you because He loves you. So, this kind of storm is to bring you to surrender, to bring you to the cross where you stop fighting God anymore and say, "God, I'm yielding and letting go.

If you look at Jonah, he finally gave in and prayed. It was a great prayer he prayed, because it brought him into repentance and restitution. When he let go, surrendered, and acknowledged the goodness and great power of God, it brought him to resurrection.

So, I wonder if God has been speaking in any area of your life, and the storm you're facing may just be a result of God wanting you to yield.

There are also some **natural storms** that come in life. There are just some situations that come because we live in a sinful and fallen world. Earthquakes, tornadoes, and landslides happen just because. It's not that God pushed that rock down the mountain and caused the landslide that took out half the town. There are things that just happen.

People do stuff—sometimes, stupid stuff. You are driving down the road, and someone crosses the line because they were texting while driving and, boom, an accident happens.

It doesn't mean that the devil made it all happen or that God was trying to get your attention and punish you. It is just because we live in a fallen world, and in this fallen world, stuff happens. Romans 8:23 says that the whole world is groaning because of sin in the world, and we live in that world.

The question we should ask, then, is: "What do we need to do to walk through this storm?" And, more importantly, "How can I glorify God in this storm?" Our natural reaction is to pass judgment or blame God in the storm. Instead, we should find how we can bring grace, the goodness of God, and the life of God into our situations.

We have to get to the place where we say, "God, give me the grace to stand in the middle of this storm and prevail." The Bible says, *"By faith and endurance we inherit promises of God."* At all times, we must learn how to stand and to bring the grace of God into a difficult circumstance. Now that's part of being a Kingdom-minded Christian.

We show our strength by finding a way to bring goodness into the storm, to overcome evil with good, and to show blessing when we are being cursed. Not by looking around and complaining.

In the natural storm you're going through, no one may be to blame. It might just be something to grow you, to allow you to get stronger.

There can be some storms that are brought about

through **spiritual warfare**. When we are pushing forward to fulfill God's purpose and plan, there will be situations that rise up to try to cause havoc. You will see with it little things that happen when people are pressing deep into God's plan and purpose. Power failures, equipment failures, difficulties, setbacks of all kinds, and even miscommunication. Sometimes it's little stuff, and sometimes it's bigger.

The sad part of this parable is found in verse 38, and it is a direct reflection of our hearts when we are in the midst of a storm. The disciples were filled with fear and did not respond well. And where was Jesus? SLEEPING! Jesus was seemingly unconcerned about their storm. They even accused Him of "not caring." They were blinded to the Kingdom realities. They looked for someone to blame for the storm instead of knowing and understanding and acting upon what must be done. They lacked the spiritual growth to understand what was going on. To endure the storms of life, we must learn and grow strong in our walk and our faith.

Jesus demonstrated how faith is exercised. He spoke directly to the storm with words of faith, words of command. He arose, rebuked the wind, and spoke to the sea. Fear quenches faith and causes storms in the mind and emotions. Our words have power, when spoken with the authority of Jesus Christ, through the Holy Spirit. Understanding the power of this requires growth and maturity of our faith.

⁴And when a great crowd was gathering and people from town after town came to him, he said in a parable, ⁵"A sower went out to sow his seed. And as he sowed, some fell along the path and was trampled underfoot, and the birds of the air devoured it. [6]And some fell on the rock, and as it grew up, it withered away, because it had no moisture. [7]And some fell among thorns, and the thorns grew up with it and choked it. [8]And some fell into good soil and grew and yielded a hundredfold." As he said these things, he called out, "He who has ears to hear, let him hear."

[9]And when his disciples asked him what this parable meant, [10]he said, "To you it has been given to know the secrets of the Kingdom of God, but for others they are in parables, so that 'seeing they may not see, and hearing they may not understand.' [11]Now the parable is this: The seed is the Word of God. [12]The ones along the path are those who have heard; then the devil comes and takes away the word from their hearts, so that they may not believe and be saved. [13]And the ones on the rock are those who, when they hear the word, receive it with joy. But these have no root; they believe for a while, and in time of testing fall away. [14]And as for what fell among the thorns, they are those who hear, but as they go on their way they are choked by the cares and riches and pleasures of life, and their fruit does not mature. [15]As for that in the good soil, they are those who, hearing the word, hold it fast in an honest and good heart, and bear fruit with patience.

(Luke 8:4–15)

Jesus uses a familiar illustration to the crowd to describe the necessity of endurance in spiritual growth. When a seed is sown, it takes root and grows to become the plant it was intended to be, as long as it endures the rigors of its environment. Plants cannot prevent difficult circumstances; they can only endure them. Harsh weather, lack of moisture, and interfering weeds make growth difficult, but fruit can still be produced if the plant endures.

While parables were often told to make truth tangible, in

Matthew 13, we find that this wasn't always the case. When His disciples question why He speaks in parables, Jesus quotes the prophet Isaiah. *"For the heart of this people has become dull, and with their ears they hear with difficulty, and they have shut their eyes, so that they would not see with their eyes and hear with their ears and understand with their heart and turn, and I would heal them"* (Matthew 13:15).

This is the case of in parable of the sower and the seed in Luke 8. The seed hits the open path, the rocky ground, the thorns, and the good soil, and Jesus describes four hearers who receive the Good News in different ways. We should examine this parable and ask ourselves, "What kind of hearer am I?"

Do we seek to really understand the Gospel? When we hear it told again and again, does it merely lay on the surface as commonplace? When our faith is put to the test, do we find ourselves putting hope in everything else but the Good News? Or, when we become anxious about the cares of this world, do we find ourselves grasping for a firm foundation that isn't there?

The seed that falls on the good soil describes a completely different reception. This hearer receives the word and *"hears it and understands it."* It doesn't stop there, however. The hearer is also known for his good works, which display a heart that has been changed. This hearer bears fruit according to what he or she has been given. *"But what was sown on the good soil—this is the one who hears the word and understands it, who indeed bears fruit and produces, this one a hundred times as much, and this one sixty, and this one thirty"* (Matthew 13:23).

Jesus emphasizes that the pursuit of Him isn't lethargic, or merely emotional, and it isn't cerebral. It involves pursuing Him with all of our being, in a posture of humility, with an ear that hears, and with a life that is changed. It involves complete surrender to His will.

The presence of suffering is necessary if we are going to grow in faith. However, suffering can also shake our faith and cause us to fall away. This is what happened to those who were like the seed that fell on the rock. They believed for a while, but in a time of testing, they too fell away. So, how do we endure the suffering of life and hold on to our faith? We must "take care how we hear." When the seed is sown, the soil must be ready to receive it.

Jeremiah 17:7-8 reads, "*Blessed is the man who trusts in the Lord, whose trust is the Lord. He is like a tree planted by water, that sends out its roots by the stream, and does not fear when heat comes, for its leaves remain green, and is not anxious in the year of drought, for it does not cease to bear fruit.*"

Make Jeremiah 17 personal to you. Grow in your faith; dive into His word to seek out words of wisdom that apply to your current situation. Communicate with God through the Holy Spirit about your situation. Ask for clarity about the storm. Repent and turn back to God if necessary. Seek His power to claim and declare victory over the storm if it is not your doing or His. Surrender yourself to His plan and the direction in which He wants you to go. All of this will mature you and grow you right out of the storm.

DISCUSSION QUESTIONS

1) When you face a challenge, what do you tell yourself?

_____

_____

_____

2) List 2 things/new adventures that you'd like to do or accomplish, but have never done. (Now is the time to begin to step out of your comfort zone and do them in faith.)

_____

_____

_____

TRAINING PLAN

Pain during and after a workout is necessary. It is the tearing down and building up of muscle that creates growth. The same is necessary if we are going to grow in faith. However, this process can also shake our faith and cause us to fall away.

This is what happened to those who were like the seed that fell on the hardened soil. They believed for a while but in a time of testing they fell away. So, how do we endure this pain of life and hold on to our faith? We must "take care how we hear." When the seed is sown, the soil must be ready to receive it.

1. Ask God to give you a new heart that receives His word - Ezekiel 36:26-27

2. "Put away all filthiness and rampant wickedness and receive with meekness the implanted word." - James 1:21

3. Desire the word more than anything else in life - Psalm 19:10

"Blessed is the man who trusts in the Lord, whose trust is the Lord. He is like a tree planted by water, that sends out its roots by the stream, and does not fear when heat comes, for its leaves remain green, and is not anxious in the year of drought, for it does not cease to bear fruit." - Jeremiah 17:7-8

CHAPTER 8
GODLINESS

"Whatever you do, do all to the glory of God."
1 Corinthians 10:31

The next component of building a strong faith from Peter's list is called godliness.

This quality describes a life directed toward God due to a deep honor and respect for our Creator. According to the New Testament, godliness can be seen through our outward appearance and actions. However, not everyone who looks godly is truly living a life directed toward God.

This is similar to an athlete who wears a jersey representing his team, but does not compete with the purpose of honoring his team. Wearing a jersey does not make someone part of the team. Some athletes are focused on their individual performance above the teams' performance. A committed member of the team will proudly honor the team he or she serves. This is the heart of godliness.

> *"For although they knew God, they did not honor him as God or give thanks to him, but they became futile in their thinking, and their foolish hearts were darkened"* (Romans 1:21).

This is a pretty sobering statement. It is hard for us to believe that someone could know God and not honor Him. Yet, if we look at the definition of honor, we quickly see how we have fallen short. To honor someone is to recognize their worth and value by appropriate attitudes and actions, to give someone a place of importance or priority in life.

> *"And whatever you do, in word or deed, do everything in the name of the Lord Jesus, giving thanks to God the Father through him. Wives, submit to your husbands, as is fitting in the Lord. Husbands, love your wives, and do not be harsh with them. Children, obey your parents in everything, for this pleases the Lord. Fathers, do not provoke your children, lest they become discouraged. Bondservants, obey in everything those who are your earthly masters, not by way of eye-service, as people-pleasers, but with sincerity of heart, fearing the Lord. Whatever you do, work heartily, as for the Lord and not for men, knowing that from the Lord you will receive the inheritance as your reward. You are serving the Lord Christ. For the wrongdoer will be paid back for the wrong he has done, and there is no partiality"* (Colossians 3:17-25).

Every role described in this passage (husband/wife, parent/child, employer/employee) is properly accomplished when directed in honor to God. To live our lives "in the name of the Lord Jesus Christ" is to honor Him in all we do.

God is worthy to be honored because of who He is.

Revelation 4:11 states, *"Worthy are you, our Lord and God, to receive glory and honor and power, for you created all things, and by your will they existed and were created."*

Knowing that the Lord is worthy to be honored, how do we honor God? The simple answer to that question is the answer to another question: "Who has the highest priority in your life, and who do you seek to please the most?"

If the answer isn't God, then you are not honoring Him throughout your life. Thus, we need to make a strong effort to follow and take hold of His purpose and priorities and to praise Him in all aspects of our lives.

God has as an eternal purpose for each one of us. Unfortunately, many people feel that we came from a random act of chance, a series of mutations that led to the human race. They think that the choices in our lives are just by chance. This has allowed many people to have different views on life, but we all ask the same question: "Why am I here?"

Ephesians 1:4 tells us that, *"God chose us before the foundation of the world."* God's purpose for us was set in motion before creation. Our lives are part of God's sovereign purpose. Think about how you came to a relationship in Christ. God reaches out to each of us personally and draws us to Him and salvation. The reason is that God is interested in our personal life and development. He has prepared activities for us to accomplish that are uniquely suited for our personality, gifts, passions, experiences and life situations.

God has a purpose for you! He created you to live it out.

He has called us to live out His practical purpose in life with passion.

> "I appeal to you therefore, brothers, by the mercies of God, to present your bodies as a living sacrifice, holy and acceptable to God, which is your spiritual worship. Do not be conformed to this world, but be transformed by the renewal of your mind, that by testing you may discern what is the will of God, what is good and acceptable and perfect" (Romans 12:1-12).

When you accomplish what God calls you to do, your life honors Him and you become fulfilled. It shouldn't matter what others do. Do what God calls you to do! Romans 12 tells us that we should make ourselves available, to be ready to aid or assist others. As you make yourself available for God to express His life and purpose through you, you will discover His perfect will for your life.

When you take the simple activities of life and do them as an act of worship, God is honored and your life has purpose. When that happens, you can do all things with excellence that honors God. And, according to the author of Colossians, chapter 3, verse 23, *"Whatsoever you do, do heartily to the Lord, knowing that from the Lord you will receive the reward of the inheritance."*

Once we know we were created with a purpose, we can honor God by pursuing His priorities in our lives. Matthew 6:20-24 states, *"Where your treasure is, there will your heart be."* Whatever we value and invest in, our hearts become involved in as well. If we value materialistic things, such as our jobs or the ways of this world, we cannot value what God has given and provided to us. We need to put His Kingdom and His purpose for our lives first. This is how we prioritize our lives to honor Him.

It's funny how often in our busy lives we always find time for what we really want to do. We rush around our day, fitting in almost everything, but we neglect the one thing we should be putting first. Where you spend your time and money reveals what is really important to you. Are you sowing into your church and mission ground or into your hobbies and the latest gadgets? Are you playing golf and watching *Sports Center*, or are you being filled by God's Word and investing in your spiritual growth? Kudos to you, the one currently reading this book. It confirms that you have a priority to grow spiritually.

Your life's priorities can also be defined by what you worry about. This worry can also you to become anxious. Your life becomes consumed on that issue instead of the One onto whom we can *"cast all anxiety and fears."* Anxieties and concerns divide our hearts and minds, unless we yield to God's care.

Our priorities can also become our obsessions or ambitions. Are you so focused on the next raise, the next jump in leadership at church, or the next promotion at work? Jesus said to seek first God's Kingdom. His rule and His priorities should be first in our lives. His priorities are found in the Great Commission. *"Go ye and…"* (Mark 12:30-31). As we focus on Him, we discover that His priories are found in His word and by listening to the Holy Spirit

Jesus asked His disciples, *"How can you believe, when you receive glory from one another and do not seek the glory that comes from the only God?"* God created us to desire the things that He desires. He desires honor and praise from us. Thus, we have a desire for honor and praise, a desire to feel valued. However, God should be the One who makes us feel valued and honored, but we too often seek the approval and praise of people.

Seeking the approval of people leads to disappointment or offense. We get hurt emotionally when we do not receive it, and then it distorts our priorities and attention from God. I have seen too many pastors walk off the stage feeling empty because they are seeking the approval of the congregation rather than knowing that they are serving God and that He honors their work. When we take our focus off of God, it erodes a life of faith and trust in God.

Galatians 1:10 gives us a sobering gauge on our priorities. *"For am I now seeking the approval of man, or of God? Or am I trying to please man? If I were still trying to please man, I would not be a servant of Christ."* If we live to please men, then we will not be servants of Christ. Let go of your desire to be praised and recognized by people. If it comes, then it will mean so much more. If it doesn't, it's not a big deal. In the grand scheme of things, we should only be looking for God's approval.

When we do that, it places Him in the highest position of honor in our lives. It means that we can stand up and speak out for God without fear. For *"God who sees in secret will reward [us] openly"* (Matthew 6:4).

We have an opportunity to live every day in honor to God with gratitude, integrity, and enthusiasm. Colossians 3:17 says, *"And whatever you do, in word or deed, do everything in the name of the Lord Jesus, giving thanks to God the Father through him."* Honor God in everything you do. Verse 22 goes on to state that we should live with integrity by *"obey[ing] in everything those who are your earthly masters, not by way of eye-service, as people-pleasers, but with sincerity of heart, fearing the Lord."* But most importantly, *"Whatever you do, work heartily, as for the Lord and not for men."*

DISCUSSION QUESTIONS

1) Define godliness. Would you say that it is always your first desire to live a life of godliness?

2) In what ways are you showing God that you trust him in all areas of your life?

3) In what ways are you not?

TRAINING PLAN

We have opportunity to live every day in honor to God.

1 Corinthians 10:31 instructs us in "whatever you do, do all to the glory of God"

Read Colossians 3:17-23.

Take time to journal how you have been living with gratitude (verse 17), integrity (verse 22), and enthusiasm (verse 23). Are you living a life that is giving glory to God every day?

CHAPTER 9
UNITY

> *"For out of the abundance of the heart the mouth speaks"*
> Matthew 12:34

In many translations, **unity** is translated as brotherly love, or brotherly affection. This is not figurative brother-like love, but the love of those united together in Christian brotherhood, or the body of Christ.

Unity in faith in the body of Christ, creates strength to build the Kingdom of God. Through spiritual training, we aim to develop functional strength. We make ourselves strong in order to build something for the future. But, we really have two choices in this world. We can either use our strength to build our own personal Kingdom, or we can share our strength with others to build the Kingdom of Christ. The New Testament speaks frequently of *"building one another up."* This means that we have an opportunity to add strength to one another.

One of the most practical ways in which we can develop unity is to add strength through our words. Corrupt talk, or a foul mouth, is not simply filled with four-letter words. The Scriptures forbid words that tear others down rather than build them up. Psalm 34:13 states, "Keep your **tongue** from evil and your lips from speaking deceit." The words we speak and agree with shape our present and determine our future and, more importantly, the future of those around us. The heart of true unity comes from speaking life and destiny into others' lives. Since God has demonstrated His grace toward us, we must seek to share this grace with others.

> [25] *Therefore, having put away falsehood, let each one of you speak the truth with his neighbor, for we are members one of another.* [26] *Be angry and do not sin; do not let the sun go down on your anger,* [27] *and give no opportunity to the devil.* [28] *Let the thief no longer steal, but rather let him labor, doing honest work with his own hands, so that he may have something to share with anyone in need.* [29] *Let no corrupting talk come out of your mouths, but only such as is good for building up, as fits the occasion, that it may give grace to those who hear.* [30] *And do not grieve the Holy Spirit of God, by whom you were sealed for the day of redemption.* [31] *Let all bitterness and wrath and anger and clamor and slander be put away from you, along with all malice.* [32] *Be kind to one another, tenderhearted, forgiving one another, as God in Christ forgave you. (Ephesians 4:25-32)*

The Bible says to put a stop to negative talk and rather practice and make it a habit to speak words that will actually edify and build up the world and the environment around us instead of tear down. This practice will minister grace and impart empowerment to those around us. We can empower people through words we speak, or we can cut them down.

down. We can cause them to live, or we can cause them to wither and die. Words have the power to change lives.

The words we agree with and the words we speak shape our future. Our words have tremendous power — they reveal who we are.

You see, you can put on an act and do all kinds of things, but after a little while of speaking, your words will show who you are because your words come out of your heart.

Matthew 12:34 tells us that out of the abundance of the heart, the mouth speaks. Whatever is in your heart will overflow and come out your mouth. Then you'll find out exactly what really is in your heart.

So I know we go to church, we sing happy songs, we love Jesus. It's a wonderful feeling and it's beautiful. We feel the presence of God. But when you are on your way to your job on Monday, stuck in traffic, or you are rushing back to get to the office from your lunch break and are a bit abrupt with the taxi driver, what words are coming out of your mouth?

It's not just the words you say; it's the impact or the feeling they create. Jesus said the words: "I speak, they are spirit, and they are life." When Jesus speaks words, they impart something of a spirit nature. That's why the first words that were recorded were spoken by God, and creation occurred. Your words can create something, so whatever is in your heart is creating something. For example, if you're constantly critical of your husband or constantly critical of your wife, constantly speaking and giving voice to negative things, you are creating a very sad marriage. You're actually creating a future that you then have to live with.

Your words are creating an atmosphere, an environment, which will either sustain your life and nourish you or will cause you to wither like a plant without water.

Words. People want words. We need words. Even Jesus said in Matthew 4:4 that, *"man shall not live by bread alone."* In other words, food is not enough to sustain us. **Our soul needs words—words that love, words that encourage, words that build, and prophetic words that speak destiny.**

There's a generation dying because there are no fathers to speak words of encouragement, love, faith, and destiny. Without these words, people get lost. They don't know where to go. They're looking for something, so they look in the bottle, they look in drugs, they look in the cell phone, they look on the Internet, they look with games, and they look with high-speed cars. They're looking for something, but what they need are creative words to shape destiny.

You and I have a unique ability to be able to create with our mouth, not only in our own life, but also in the lives of others. Whatever words you agree with, whatever you're speaking, is creating a world around you. What kind of atmosphere are you creating?

A spiritual atmosphere is created by the words you speak. Either you invite the Holy Spirit and the angels of God into your house, and the words you speak are cultivating that atmosphere, or you invite demons into the house that will cause all kinds of other things to enter into your house, like anger, malice, deceit, disharmony, etc. All of these things break the unity that should be established for a spiritual atmosphere.

How do I get into a relationship with God? Words. How did you get married? Words. Words establish the covenant. When those words are witnessed and were written down, they became a binding covenant. Words on earth are listened to in the heavens. When you speak cursing words, demons are just waiting, and they become empowered to begin to operate. You can also speak words into your own life. You can agree with negative words about your own life, and as you begin to give voice to them, they will cause demons to operate against you. You can agree with the words other people speak, and then when you agree with them and begin to repeat them, what happens then is that demons are unleashed. Agreement on the earth, and then giving voice to what we've agreed with, activates things in the supernatural realm. We have to understand the importance of this in our lives and those around us.

In Numbers 13, twelve people went into the Promised Land and God showed them some wonderful things. Unfortunately, ten of them came back, and what was in their hearts was negativity, and it flowed out. They began to say things like, "We can't do it! We can't, it's too hard. There are giants and big walled cities." Out of their hearts, they were basically saying, "I know God is good, but this is too big for Him." Fear was in their hearts and out came those words.

And the very words they spoke determined their future. They were not able to enter and take what God had promised them. God said, "I've heard what you spoke and I will come into agreement with you, so it's not going to happen." Let that sink in. How many times have you spoken death onto your dreams or spoken death onto someone else's dream?

Caleb said, "Our God is mighty! If He is with us, we are well able." Joshua said, "I've brought word, as was in my heart." One group of people looked at the circumstances, and doubt, fear, negativity, and feeling sorry for themselves arose, and they agreed with it. Once they agreed with it, they spoke it, and that was their destiny.

Are we agreeing with what God says about you or what others say about you?

Joshua, the Bible says, agreed with the Lord. He said, "I brought word as was in my heart." What was in his heart? That his God was with them, and they were well able. See, what gets in your heart is what finds expression through your mouth. Hence the heart has to be cleansed because that's the source of the trouble with the tongue. You can stop talking, but in the end, you've still got stuff in your heart that will only be removed through a repentant and surrendered heart.

You may have rejection. Rejection has a voice. You may have fear; fear has a voice. You may have shame, or self-pity. These things have voices. If you hear those voices speaking and agree with them, you will come into alignment and start to speak. I can't do anything. Nobody loves me.

You've come into agreement with those words, and you have all those things because you have agreed to them in your heart.

When demons get into a person's life, first of all, they

speak to that person. Eve came into agreement with the Devil's words, and then she began to speak them. That is when the problem started. It defined her destiny. She let the Devil's words come into her heart. Once the words got in there, and she agreed with him and gave voice to them, then her destiny was set.

I don't know **who** you have been agreeing with or **what** you've been agreeing with. You could be agreeing with negatives that have been spoken into you life; perhaps someone spoke over you, saying that you're no good or that you'll never amount to anything. Now, if you agree with that, then that will actually begin to reflect through your life and your mouth, and it'll shape your future. You must understand that **what you agree with and begin to speak will shape and create your future**. We have to break the agreement with the negatives that we've been listening to over the years, begin to meditate on them, come into agreement with what God says, and reflect His Word into our world.

Now, the problem is, if our experiences have been really bad, it actually is a leap of faith to abandon our old way of speaking and thinking and start to think and speak the way that God wants us to think and speak. You've made room for the Word of God and the Spirit of God to move.

See, if we begin to say, "Well, I can't do that" because someone has spoken over our lives phrases such as, "You're dumb, you're stupid, you're thickheaded, you'll never come to anything," then we begin to agree with these words. We are wounded by those words and have come into agreement with it. Then, God begins to come into our lives and talks about our destiny, and we have a hard time believing His truth and

His word for our lives because we are still in agreement with the past words spoken onto our lives.

Break the agreement. Resolve the past and become empowered in the present. Then your future will begin to reflect what God has given to. But it takes a first step. That first step sometimes means that we have to forgive people who have hurt us. Then we need to cancel our agreement with the words and the thoughts and begin to speak something different.

What are you agreeing with? What words are you listening to in your heart that are negative and defeat-filled words? You're reflecting them into your environment. You have to cancel its power completely. Say to yourself, "I'm going to deal with this thing at its root, and the root is always in the heart and expressed through the mouth." God wants us to come into agreement with Him.

We have the Word of God, so God wants us day and night to have His word come into our hearts about who we are, what we're called to do, what we can do, and what we can be. We need to give voice to it!

God's Word says: You're a child of God! You're the daughter and the son of a king! You're royal family, destined to rule, destined to reign. **You have a destiny!**

Hebrews 3:1 states that Jesus is the High Priest of our confession. The word confession means the act of speaking what God is saying about us and our circumstances. What you need to do is to agree with what God says about you, about your family, about your marriage, about your finances, and about your world because if you agree with Him, you position yourself to come up to actually see Him work on your behalf.

The Scriptures say that Jesus is the High Priest. The High Priest's role is to go into the presence of God, intercede on behalf of others, begin to receive blessing, and bring it out to the people. So, when Jesus goes before the Father, He has something to go with. It's your confession! And not just talk and talk and confessing about your sins. When we confess our sins, it positions us to be forgiven, provided that you believe that Jesus died on the cross for you.

But God wants us to access the realm of the supernatural, so He has to have something to work with. We need to start confessing God's Word about us and our situation.

People are waiting for you to break through. All around you, there's someone waiting for you to break through from negativity. Maybe there are some relationships you need to cut off. Not all friendships and relationships help us achieve what God wants. The devil is well able to send people into your life, people full of negativity who just eat out what God is trying to do, and you don't even know it. Maybe you have some sense of false loyalty or you're holding onto those people, thinking that this is going to change them. If they haven't changed in five years, what makes you think that they're going to change now? What's been happening to you, all those years while that negativity's been getting into your ears?

Ask the Holy Spirit to reveal what is in your heart, the

place where you have embraced negative thoughts, doubts, despair, unbelief, or self-pity. The place where you have listened to gossip, listened to rumors, and focused on negative things. Have Him show you where the things are. Every time He shows you something, repent from it. Break your agreement with it and declare the things that God says about you.

Give up the stuff that's filling you with despair and hopelessness. Then flee from it. Some people can't even begin a day without having to look at the news to see what's happening. Spoiler alert: it's all bad because that is what makes the news interesting. You rarely hear about the good stuff, even though it's happening all around. The main channels are concerned with the negativity because it's what sells. People are absorbed with it. So why listen to that? Why watch that and come into agreement about what mass media says about the world around you?

God wants us to change us on the inside. The Bible says that if you believe with your heart and confess with your mouth that Christ is Lord, salvation comes to you. If that's how our faith starts, then that's how it continues. Believe that God provides for you. Believe that God comes through for you. Let your heart dwell and meditate on His word until it truly is rooted in your heart.

Refuse to agree with the doubts and the negatives. Begin to speak God's truth day by day. Believe that He is your portion. Believe that He is all you need to fulfill your life. As you believe, and **as you begin to declare those things, you will start to make a way in your life for the Spirit of God to move afresh**. Out of your heart, new words will arise that will bring grace and healing to the lives of those around you, to unite what was once divided in your life and in the relationships of others.

Reflect on Christ's example of building up through His words as He tells us who we are in John 15:12-17 and who we can be in John 17:20-26.

John 15:12-17

[12]"This is my commandment, that you love one another as I have loved you. [13]Greater love has no one than this, that someone lay down his life for his friends. [14]You are my friends if you do what I command you. [15]No longer do I call you servants, for the servant does not know what his master is doing; but I have called you friends, for all that I have heard from my Father I have made known to you. [16]You did not choose me, but I chose you and appointed you that you should go and bear fruit and that your fruit should abide, so that whatever you ask the Father in my name, he may give it to you. [17]These things I command you, so that you will love one another.

John 17:20-26

[20]"I do not ask for these only, but also for those who will believe in me through their word, [21]that they may all be one, just as you, Father, are in me, and I in you, that they also may be in us, so that the world may believe that you have sent me. [22]The glory that you have given me I have given to them, that they may be one even as we are one, [23]I in them and you in me, that they may become perfectly one, so that the world may know that you sent me and loved them even as you loved me. [24]Father, I desire that they also, whom you have given me, may be with me where I am, to see my glory that you have given me because you loved me before the foundation of the world. [25]O righteous Father, even though the world does not know you, I

know you, and these know that you have sent me. [26]I made known to them your name, and I will continue to make it known, that the love with which you have loved me may be in them, and I in them."

DISCUSSION QUESTIONS

1) What does God's Word say about the power of our words?

_____

_____

_____

2) What words does God use to describe you?

_____

_____

_____

3) We discussed serving others earlier in the book, and speaking words of affirmation and encouragement is one of the ways we serve one another. Name 3 people you can serve this week just with words of encouragement and affirmation?

_____

_____

_____

TRAINING PLAN

Journal your experiences and relationships that have contributed greatly to your personal strengths.

Write out some of the false beliefs and lies the enemy has told you about yourself. Rewrite those beliefs as statements of truth about how God sees you.

Example

False statement: I am not lovable because of my past.

True statement: Because of Jesus' death on the cross for my sins, my past does not make me who I am today. I am loved by my heavenly Father.

CHAPTER 10
LOVE

> *"Love the Lord your God with all your heart...*
> *love your neighbor as yourself"*
> Matthew 22:36-40

Many times we quantify our actions by our ability to do them efficiently. This is true in fitness and any other activity that produces a goal. Have you noticed what happens when you do not hit your goals? Have you ever experienced a loss of passion for achieving your goals for whatever reason? Maybe it became too hard. Maybe others told you it wasn't possible. Maybe you believed the voice that said, "You never finished anything; you are not good enough; you cannot win."

Over time, we lose our motivation and end up coasting through life because we don't see the fruit of our hard work fast enough. You might have seen it in organizations or athletic teams around you. They've lost the motivation to push through the hard times, and as a result get discouraged, frustrated, and angry, and just give up. However, working hard and pushing through, especially in times of difficulty or when we have lost the passion to continue, is the best time to put our faith in God to the test. The provider of our faith is Christ, and therefore when we are weary, He makes us strong. Our pursuits should not be about ourselves, but about the glory we give to God through them. Through His love we can do so many things.

Our faith lacks strength when we stop pursuing its source. When we receive the **love** of Christ, we are given a strength that can never be taken away. We have been given the ability to do good works, along with a motivation that cannot be removed by any circumstances. **We have been given purpose outside of ourselves.**

But many of us have lost that motivation to pursue our purpose.

If we are honest with ourselves, a big factor for our loss of motivation is that we have forgotten to love ourselves. Did you know that how you relate to and treat yourself has a big impact on how you relate to and treat others? Jesus told His followers, *"Love the Lord your God with all your heart… love your neighbor as yourself"* (Matthew 22:36-40).

So, what do you believe about yourself? Do you love yourself? Do you accept yourself as God made you, or do you base your thoughts on what others have told you? Do you agree with God about your identity and your value?

What do you say about yourself? Try saying, "I am a

child of God, and I am loved and accepted."

Was that easy to say, but harder to believe? Say it again. "I am a child of God, and I am loved and accepted." Do you agree? If you don't agree with yourself, then maybe you need to agree with God. Maybe you need to say the same thing that God says about you. God's Word says to *"see what manner of love the Father has bestowed on us that we should be called the children of God"* (1 John 3:1).

Now say, "I am a child of God, and I am loved and accepted. God is my Father and I belong to God. God places immense value on me." Romans 8:15 says that, *"you have received the Spirit of adoption whereby you cry Abba Father. The Spirit bears witness with our spirit, we are the children of God."*

Even while it sounds great, and it's in God's Word, maybe you are still having a hard time believing that truth. Loving yourself can be difficult if there has been destructive influences from others. It's amazing how we can allow someone else's lies about us to become truths in our own lives. Have you ever had someone say that they don't love you? Maybe it wasn't words; maybe it was their actions or attitudes toward you.

In order to love yourself, you need to first limit and set boundaries of destructive influences in your life. If you permit others to influence what you believe about yourself, then you are actually disagreeing with what God says about your value. The first step to loving yourself is to identify things that are trying to come into your life. The most destructive influences in our lives enter in through our eyes and ears.

- What we hear: negative people, complaining, gossiping, our thoughts…

- What we see: television, Internet, social media, books…

The first Psalm states that, "B*lessed is the man who walks not in the couple of the wicked."*

Tell yourself, "I'm not going to walk with sinners, sit in the seat of the scornful, or point the finger at other people and mock what they're doing." It's actually about making a stand, of setting boundaries around your life.

Now, when it comes to many people that come into our lives, we can love them, embrace them, welcome them, and talk with them. We can help them, but we cannot let their negativity—and their negative influences—come in and invade our lives. We will always find people that we come across who are very negative.

When we talk with them, they complain, and they often continue to complain. They're critical. They are always complaining about someone or putting another person down. They are talking negatively about the boss, the government, or their church.

We find people who are demanding. They're putting pressure on us. They say, "You have to do this; you have to do that," and if you don't, then we feel that we are not worthy. We meet people who are bitter. Sometimes we can see it on their faces, but we definitely hear it in their words.

Sometimes, we meet people who are angry. Sometimes, we meet people who are seductive or defiling. Now, when we meet people like that, there are spiritual influences that flow and can impact us.

The Bible is very clear when it tells us that bad communications corrupt our lifestyle, so we have to really watch what people say to us and make a stand about things that are destructive.

It's not such a hard thing. If you find that someone is complaining, do you speak to that person about it without letting it negatively affect you? If someone is critical, do you ask this person if he or she is hearing the truth or just hearsay? We do not have to go along with complaints and criticisms we hear from people. A common quote helps explain these types of situations clearly: "Hurting people hurt people." We need to avoid allowing these people to have such influence over our thoughts with their words.

Our eyes also allow negative influences into our lives. Psalm 101:3 instructs us to *"not set before [our] eyes anything that is worthless."* Influences like the media, entertainment, books, TV, computers, and the Internet can so easily defile ourselves. These are not bad inventions, but we have to discern what to allow our eyes to see. Job said, *"I made a covenant with my eyes, not to look upon a woman."* Why? Because where our eyes go, our hearts will go also.

In order to love yourself, you need to make a commitment to yourself that you will begin to guard yourself from what can come into you, including visual media. Otherwise, your standards about yourself will lower and be eroded. You won't even know what you've got; you're not loving yourself when you do that. Actually, you're abusing yourself when you do that because your value is not going up; your value is going down. Why is it going down? Because what God gave into you is now being eroded.

You need to resolve the negative influences that are inside you and that operate in your own life. If you love yourself, then be committed to personal growth. When you resolve those negative influences from your past and present, you will then love and value yourself.

In 2 Chronicles 29, God's Word talks about King Hezekiah. He was a reformer of sorts. When he became King, in the first year of his reign, he opened the doors of the house of the Lord and repaired them. He spoke to the Levites—the ones who were supposed to keep the temple pure and holy—and told them to get the house of the Lord in order. They were told to *"sanctify the house of the Lord God of your fathers, carry the rubbish out of the holy place, for our fathers have trespassed, and done evil in the eyes of the Lord our God."* See, they shut up the doors, put out the lamps, and they hadn't burned incense or burnt offerings. So, the priests went to the inner part of the house of the Lord to cleanse it and brought out all the debris they found in the temple of the Lord to the court of the house of God.

Apply this to your life. You and I are the house of the Lord; we represent the body of Christ (Ephesians 5:30). We must first look at the gates, where we allow things to enter. We need to look at the areas of access where things come in and out and repair these areas. The gates are always representations of entranceways. It says that Hezekiah restored them and covered them with gold. He restored the glory of God's presence into the gates. If there have been things that you have allowed to enter in, then take the time to "repair the gates" and restore them to their original glory. Remove the influences that affect how you see yourself. Stop watching the shows that have a negative effect on you. Shut down the negative relationships in your life that do not feed you.

Discover from the Word of God, learn what He hates and what He loves, and **begin to love the things He loves and hate the things He hates.** Begin to align your life along that path. The result? You begin to receive the love of God, and then you love and feel loved.

Then Hezekiah went into the inner place and cleansed out what was there. In the very same way, we need to resolve things that are going on in our lives, some of which have been there for years. This is probably the toughest area to work through, and it may require some deep reflection and even counseling. Pain is usually physical. We can feel it, see it, and know when it happens. Often, with the wounds in our soul, we're not so aware of the damage that's been caused, so we don't usually take the effort to do anything. We may not even know there is a hurt, but it has influenced our belief of ourselves.

Deep down, there may be inherited curses, family patterns, that are operating in your family. Are there fears that cause you to feel intimidated? Bring them out, and get them sorted out. Has someone spoke cursing over your life? What about trauma and things that have affected you emotionally?

If there are negative issues eroding your life, love yourself enough to get some help. Ask someone to help you bring resolution to it. Why live in defeat and bondage when you don't need to? An interesting passage in the Old Testament states that God told His people to "*drive these enemies out of the land, because if you don't, they'll be a prick in your eye, and a thorn in your flesh*" (*Numbers 33:52*). After you become a Christian, what you leave unaddressed in your life becomes a "prick in your eye"; it affects your vision and becomes a "thorn in your flesh."

God values you, and He made provision for these issues to be dealt with. He made provision for your grief to be cast out, and for every area of your life to be healed and restored. It's His plan to restore you, so if you are going to agree with God that you are valuable, also agree with God that He has provided for your wholeness; then, pursue it. Love yourself enough to deal with your issues. Instead of blaming God for these things, discover the redemption He has made available. Build back the bond and love with God.

What you focus on influences what happens in your life.

The Bible says that if you are around someone who is angry, you'll become angry. The people you're hanging out with, or the people you associate with and make your friends, influence you. Why not take the time to build a relationship with God, to become intimate with Him, to listen to Him, to build a life that pleases Him.

We feel loved because we have a source that no one can see. It's an invisible source. Now, God can also love us through people, so we need to be connected to people who are positive, people who are encouraging, people in the body of Christ who are loving and can help us and encourage us. We need those kinds of relationships. Why? Because that's one way through which God loves us and helps us to feel of value.

God provides the freedom and the ability for us to remove any negative influences in our lives. But we have to do our part as well. Remember Jacob? Jacob wrestled and fought. There was a whole struggling over issues in his life, and then, out of that encounter, he was changed completely. God even changed his name. **Encounters with God change you. Love yourself enough to pursue God, and seek encounters with Him, particularly encounters where you hear His word for yourself.**

What a tremendous thing — that you would love yourself enough to agree with what God says about you, who you are, what you can do, and what the possibilities are for your life. That you would love yourself enough to put a boundary up and say no to people treating you badly, or to other things happening which are negative. That you'd love yourself enough to say, "No more," to some of the things which are affecting your life and begin to deal with them. That you'd love yourself enough to say, "I want to be friends with the most wonderful person because I want to become like Him."

As you do that, you begin to find that your life changes; everything in you changes. You see yourself differently; you see people differently. It all starts with a choice: to love yourself. And in doing so, Matthew 22:36-40 comes to life:

"Love the Lord your God with all your heart…love your neighbor

as yourself."

Jesus stated that all the Law and the prophets are summarized in those two commands. The Bible is about love. It's about revealing the nature of God, God's love for us, and our love for Him in response.

It's important that we experience God, not just know about Him, but to experience Him, and have encounters with Him so we can hear His voice.

That's the fuel for the fire. That's the fuel to keep us alive, but encounters with God are always to lead us to mission. Love always has an outworking, or a practical expression. How do we know love? This can be clearly seen in 1 John 3:16:

> *"By this we know love, that he laid down his life for us, and we ought to lay down our lives for the brothers. And whoever has this world's goods, and sees his brother in need, and shuts up his heart from him, how does the love of God abide in him? My little children, let us not love in word or in tongue, but in deed and in truth. And by this we know we're of the truth, and shall assure our hearts before Him."*

This is what love is about. **Love is seen in what Jesus does.** Jesus, the Bible tells us, is filled with the love, filled with the compassion of God, but you can't have a heart full of love and have nothing overflow. If you have the love of God in you, then there must be an expression of it some way. Jesus overflows.

How did He express the love of God while on the earth? He expressed it tangibly. He applied the anointing of the power of God to minister to needs of people. He connected with people where they were. He demonstrated acceptance of people. He discovered the needs that people had by listening to and interacting with them. Wherever He met with people, He allowed His life routines to be interrupted so that the needs of people could be met. He demonstrated what love looks like. Love is incredibly practical.

He loves us so much that He laid down His life for us. He sacrificed His life. Ephesians 5:1 says, *"Be followers of God, even as Christ loved us and gave an example to us follow His example."* If He laid His life down, then that's the example we ought to follow; we ought to lay down our lives for our brothers.

However, because of our flesh, the opposite often happens. When we see someone in need, instead of acting out of love, we often start judging. We look at what others are doing or not doing. This is reality. We need to define our Christian walk using Jesus as the model. As He walked is how we should walk. As He handled people, is how we should handle people. God wants to reveal what Jesus is like through us, and He can't do it unless we engage with people with love.

You'll find that your experiences of God are also connected to your experiences with people, as well as how we interact and work with people. 1 John 3:16 states, *"Whoever has this world's goods and sees his brother in need and shuts up his heart from him, how does the love of God abide in him?"* The key is seeing someone in need.

Now, there are more needs than you can minister to, so you don't have to minister to every need there is. You're not responsible to meet every need. Even Jesus didn't meet every need. He walked in and out of the temple week by week, and nevertheless, there was a cripple there. He never healed that cripple. He was motivated and directed by an inspiration from His Father.

Most of the time, when we see someone in need, we think to ourselves, "Someone ought to do something about that." When it tugs at your heart, then the person who needs to do something is you. The person who ought to do something about it is you because you have seen the need. We are not required to meet the needs of everyone. What we are required to do is to not shut our heart when we see a person in need.

One of the problems with a lot of exposure to TV is that we see a lot of world news, violence, destruction, and all the difficulties and things that happen to people. If you watch too much violence on TV, or if you play too many video games in which people are being killed, you become a spectator and your heart becomes hardened.

You can look at a need and not be moved.

So, the Bible tells us that love—the love that God is looking for—is not just about lifting our hands in worship. It goes beyond that. It actually overflows when you see someone with a need, and you begin to take initiative to connect with and help the person.

Read that 1 John 3:16 again. If you see the brother in need and have something that can supply that need, yet you shut your heart up, how can you say that the love of God is manifesting in your life?

It's important for us to maintain good works. The last chapter of Titus tells us to be careful to maintain good works, in order that we will be fruitful (Titus 3). In other words, God wants us to ensure that we're not just our talk, but that we are actually on the ground level and doing things that change the lives of those around us. Be careful to maintain good works.

Jesus was intimate with the Father, and He abounded in good works to people. He was anointed by the Holy Spirit. In Acts 10:38, we learn that Jesus was anointed by the Holy Spirit, and He went around doing good and healing all who were oppressed of the devil.

So, **our love, our relationship, our intimacy with the Father is to lead us to overflow and connect with people**. Our connections with people are where the reality, the substance, and the maturity of our Christian life is revealed, so spiritual experiences need to be connected to practical action. Isaiah had an encounter with heaven, saw the throne of God, the glory of God, heard the angels, and saw, felt, and experienced heaven. Then, coming out of that encounter, he captured the heart of God. He said, *"Lord, send me"* (Isaiah 6:8). He wanted to be part of the answer in meeting the needs of people.

The most powerful overflow of our spiritual experience is that we begin to engage with people in a different way. Spiritual experiences, revelation from the Word, and revelations of spiritual things must lead to encountering and working with people. Paul said that he had more revelation than anyone. However, he also had pressure and afflictions come against him.

One of the problems that come with this is that the greater spiritual experiences and revelation we have, the greater responsibility we have to **engage with people**.

Love that's practical, the real experience with God, and the tangible experience of God will direct us to people. We find the greatest success comes when we seek the highest good for others no matter the cost to ourselves. We are winners when we do whatever it takes to make others win. This is real strength. This is success. This is Christ in you and I.

"Love one another with brotherly affection. Outdo one another in showing honor" (Romans 12:10).

DISCUSSION QUESTIONS

1) Do you believe God's love is for you?

_____

_____

_____

2) What do you believe about yourself?

_____

_____

_____

TRAINING PLAN

In order to build your faith, speak the things over yourself that God says about you.

What was Jesus willing to do for us?

What kept Him motivated even when facing the most difficult circumstances?

What you focus on influences what happens in your life. Journal some of the areas on your life you have been focusing on. What are some of the things causing you stress? What do you lay awake at night thinking or worrying about?

List out each area of focus. Identify why that is an area of focus. What parts have you been trying to solve and what parts have you given to God to solve?

CHAPTER 11
TRAINING PLAN

> *"For while bodily training is of some value, godliness is of value in every way, as it holds promise for the present life and also for the life to come."*
> 1 Timothy 4:8

Getting stronger is not easy. You need a training plan.

With any training program, we need to know where weaknesses are in order to grow. From there, we need to have a plan and move forward. This is where things get tough. We can't just pretend through the actions. We have to be real and authentic in order to grow.

True growth and strength comes from facing our realities and not shying away from our responsibility. **God's plan is**

for us to grow, mature, represent Him, and advance His Kingdom in society. We are not to be pretenders, ineffective believers sitting in the church pew. God sent His Son to earth to represent Him. Jesus left and said, *"As the Father sent Me, now I send you."* That's a big responsibility, and I have to assume that He didn't want to send out a bunch of pretenders. A good gauge to see how authentic or mature we are can be found in the way in which we deal with the people around us.

This is my hearts cry for the Church —that every part of our lives is engaged in passionately loving God, walking in the Spirit, and it overflows to those around us.

You are probably familiar with the story of the Good Samaritan, but let's look at the last portion of the story. In summary, there was a man who had been beaten up in life and had been wounded. It says that the Samaritan went to him; he initiated action to go to the man who had been traumatically impacted by what had happened to him, and after pouring on oil and wine, set him on his horse, took him to an inn, and took care of him.

This man entered the world of someone who was traumatized, found out what was wrong in his life, and brought the life anointing of the Holy Spirit to impart, to heal, and to bring restoration to him.

All believers are called into this ministry. We are called to follow Jesus' example. Jesus said, *"The spirit of the Lord is upon Me. He's anointed Me to preach the gospel to the poor"* (Luke 4:18). Preaching the Gospel is to bring people into an encounter with the living God in order to become saved.

But God has so much more for us than that.

He has anointed us to heal the broken hearted. God wants to heal brokenness in our lives so that we can enter into meaningful relationships, for without relationships, we don't have life. That may seem very bold to stay, but think about it. We all know people who substitute things for relationships. We were made to relate to people and to God, so we have to learn to have a relationship with God.

What God wants to do with us is put into us a love that will grow us so mature that we can actually enter into the world of others and help them. The problem is, how can we enter the world of other people very successfully if we won't even enter our own world? How can we be authentic to other people if we're covering up who we really are and what's really going on? For many people, their daily walk is actually inconsistent with what they believe. We must grow stronger in our walk if we want to truly reflect Jesus in our lives.

To come into the presence of God means **to face what is really happening in our lives**.

In Genesis, we see that Adam and Eve concealed their identity, covered themselves up, and hid as a consequence of the Fall. This reaction came about as a result of Adam and Eve feeling fear and believing that God was going to punish them. So, when we look at people's lives, we see the outward part, which is like the tip of an iceberg on the surface, but below that outward part is where people really live.

If you are going to grow stronger in your relationship with God and in your ability to represent Him, you have to change on the inside. Utilize the discussion questions in each chapter as areas to reflect on. Take the time to journal the "Training Plan" topics at the end of each chapter.

Every athlete is always looking for that extra edge in competition and training. We have that extra edge through the Holy Spirit. The Holy Spirit is given to every believer, and He dwells inside us. His job is to bring to our awareness where we need to grow up. He speaks into our hearts direction and correction. And it will bring about maturity so that we can discover who we are and how to relate to others; we will live our lives and know how to fulfill our purpose. Jesus said that He would pour His spirit into us, and the Holy Spirit inside of us will be a witness. He will teach us that God is our Father, but also, that Spirit—the Holy Spirit—in us is to bring us to face realities, to face truth. If we keep covered up and hide our lives, or if we pretend that we've moved on when we haven't moved on, or if we minimize what's happening in our lives, we miss out on the opportunity to grow and fulfill what God called us to do.

The problem is that, with many exercise programs, we sometimes want to avoid growing because of the pain and sacrifice we have to endure.

In Exodus, we find the nation of Israel released from the bondage of Egyptian rule, only to be wandering through the wilderness. This is similar to our walk with Christ. **We become free from sin when we give our lives to Christ, but sometimes we still find ourselves not walking the path that Jesus walked.** We don't really like to follow the rules. God has His promises about our marriage, our family, our finances, our future, and our destiny, but we are often not willing to embrace it.

Why did a 10-day journey end up taking 40 years?

The Israelites refused to face what they needed to face in order to grow and change. God was trying to raise up a generation who had faith and courage. So, He allowed them to go through some experiences that were painful. They had an opportunity to grow. But unfortunately, they kept complaining and did not look at the opportunity to grow.

They were unable to enter into all that God had for them.

Consider your personal life now. How many things has God had for you that you refused to enter into and allow for growth? What happens is that we often delay our lives from ever progressing and accomplishing all God wants. That's why many Christians have accomplished little or nothing after years. They're still in the same place they were years ago.

God wants us to move through difficulties, pressures, stresses, and, at times, opposition in order that we grow stronger because He has many things for us in our community, our city, our nation and beyond. He allows us to go through some difficulties in order that faith might grow.

The purpose is not to be forced into changing, but being humbled enough to allow God to transform us. We have burdens and bondage that hold us back. God knows it, but we need to come to realize it as well.

He's waiting for us to acknowledge the deep-seated fear, grief, or bitterness that is buried deep inside.

God knows, but He has to take us through experiences

that allow what is in us to surface. He refines us like the refiner refining gold. He heats it until it melts and all the impurities rise to the top. He then removes all the junk at the top and keeps what is pure and usable.

Of course, being human, we want to be in control. We don't like the refining fire. It hurts too much; we don't want to revisit that pain again, we don't want to grow up, and we don't want to change. We fear the change because it's unknown, and we are not in control. But the great part is the He is in control.

What you fear will control your life, so when you feel that you're about to lose control, it's just the point when you have the chance to grow in your faith, your believing, and your trust in God.

In order to do that, you have to look deep inside. Real change requires that we be honest. Our preferred choice is to control and manipulate our external life so that we won't have to face the internal junk. Our God wants to transform what is in us and take ownership of it.

Be courageous and face the truth. Proverbs 28:13 says that if you cover your sins, you shall not prosper, but if you confess and forsake them, you find mercy. It's foolish to believe that we can cover our weakness or cover up our sin. It always has an effect in our lives. We cannot live a life of false pretense because we will not be able to prosper or move forward.

We are called to go forward, to grow from one degree of glory to another. That means we are to grow from one degree of believing God or trusting God to another. To do that, we can't cover where we're failing and making mistakes.

We need to actually do what the Bible says to do. If we confess and turn away from our sin, then we experience mercy coming into our lives. In other words, if we are aware of where we're missing it and consciously address that and put it off of our lives, we will always encounter mercy from God. He offers kindness, graciousness, and the willingness to give you another go, but the key is you have to actually own it. In the New Testament, the word 'confess' is *"homologeō"* meaning that if we will say about our lives what God is saying about them, and if we change, then He will give us grace.

But if you minimize or defend yourself, cover it up, or try and pretend that it is better than it is, then you won't find grace. You won't prosper at all. A key to growing stronger is being able to be willing to face painful truth, and it is not easy. I remember more than one time in my journey being on my knees, weeping before God over seeing and perceiving my failure and how it hurt people, seeing things in my life that were broken and needed to be repaired, and seeing things that I was lacking in. I've wept many, many times in this secret place before the Lord over those things that I had worked to try and change outside of His help. Through God's grace and mercy I was transformed by the power of the Holy Spirit and was made **stronger**, after confessing, repenting, and turning from my sin.

When you do that, you find that God pours out grace. God will help you. God will walk with you. There is humility and there is brokenness, and God is working because He's not looking at how bad it is. God is seeing the heart that will respond, and He can work with this heart. David murdered and committed adultery, lied, and did all kinds of things, but God saw a man after His heart; He could work with someone who will respond like that.

You don't have to be perfect with God; you just have to have a perfect heart. That means that you are open to respond when the Holy Spirit speaks to you. When you do that, your life can really begin to shift. If you are resistant and walled off and hard-hearted when God when speaks to you, then your life is not going to change in any kind of way. You are not growing strong at all. You're not going forward.

If you're going to grow stronger, then you need to receive grace—the kindness and the help of God. Don't beat yourself up if you've made mistakes or you have things that are not right. Just face it, deal with your part of it, and receive grace from God.

Come to him and say, "Lord help me now. Give me the strength I need; give me the wisdom I need. Show me how to handle this situation. Help me again, oh God; I've blown it again. Lord, I have blown it again, I realize what I did Lord; help me." Then, God will pour His spirit out on your heart. He will enable you to get up and move. *The steps of a good man are ordered by the Lord* (Psalm 37:23). In other words, God knows all about your failings, but the Lord upholds you and gets you back up again so that you can take your steps of faith.

He will give grace to the humble. He will lift you up. He will help you go forward, and while others are just locked where they are. Step by little step, you will be progressing forward, growing, and coming up more aware of yourself and more aware of God's grace and goodness. You will be more able to enter into the lives of other people.

God sees the heart that responds and works with it. The Holy Spirit speaks to an open heart. We won't go forward if we don't grow. Be able to receive grace; don't beat yourself up. Ask God to help you, guide you, show you, and enable you to get up. When you ask for forgiveness and help, grace and goodness will come to the humble. You will then be able to show grace to others and minister to them. We need to take responsibility to grow and change, otherwise we don't have anything to give to other people. **Don't stay where you are; step forward, move on, and step up.**

God created us to be productive, to be fruitful, and to bring increase to our lives and to the lives around us, not to just sit back and let life happen around us. He has given us the amazing opportunity to share His work here on earth, in our personal lives, and in our relationships to have an impact on His people.

By reading this book, you have discovered eight areas of your life that can help you become stronger in your walk — faith, character, knowledge, self-control, perseverance, godliness, unity, and love. By focusing on these strength fundamentals, you will get stronger.

My prayer is that you will reflect on each of these eight areas and identify the areas in which need to grow stronger. Identify what has hindered your growth in the past. Determine if there are any unresolved hurts or offenses or expectations of which you need to let go. Finally, determine what action or changes you must make to let go of these hindrances so that you can move on and grow.

Realize that God is the source of your freedom and increase, not people or circumstances. *"God is able to make all grace abound to you, so that having all sufficiency in all things at all times, you may abound in every good work"* (2 Corinthians 9:8).

God created everything. Fruit must grow and live off of the tree from which it grew. If you cut it off from that tree, it will die. That same principle is true in our lives. If we are cut off from God, our potential is aborted. We must live with Him, draw life from Him. Our need for God is not an option. We cannot flourish apart from God. Jesus shared this truth when He said to His disciples, *"He that abides in me and I in him brings forth much fruit. Without me you can do nothing."*

You need to start desiring God's best for your life. Psalm 37:4 says, *"Delight oneself in the Lord and He will give you the desires of your heart."* God plants our desires in our hearts. Our job is to recognize them and cultivate them. We need to move toward the things that we really desire by exercising faith. Jesus even told us to believe for what we ask for in prayer, and it will be ours. It requires faith, truly believing in God's best for you. We must lay aside things in our lives that confuse us or cloud our abilities to have faith in His plan for us. We must want something enough that we are willing to do something about it. Getting strong means change and adjustment, so that may mean laying aside some things now so we can have more things later.

Many athletes focus on doing the same movement repetitively, so it becomes a habit over time. In this same way, develop a habit of hearing and applying God's Word to your life. God's Word is a seed. Release His life, power, and ability in yourself through His Word. **Remember that faith comes by hearing and a willingness to be changed.** Living out our faith releases the resources of God into our situation.

Just as athletes have natural ability, God has already given you many talents and gifts. Don't focus on your lack or inability. Discover what God has already supplied you, and put it to use. God asked Moses to use what was in his hand: his walking stick.

With that tool and God's power, Moses parted the Red Sea. We have to put to use what God has given us, otherwise, it goes to waste.

Develop practical steps for your growth. Every athlete has specific goals and the steps necessary to achieve them. There are no get-rich-quick schemes in God's Kingdom. He wants us to grow stronger, but it takes sowing and reaping. There are no overnight successes, just years of labor for His Kingdom. The nation of Israel had to possess their land of inheritance little by little.

My prayer for you is that there will be a stirring in you, a stirring to begin to consider how your life can be adjusted and to grow to enjoy and express your love on a greater level. I'm praying for a release of creativity of ideas and how to bring the love of God to people. I'm asking the Lord for an increase of your anointing as well, that through your simple acts of kindness and love, the hearts of others will be transformed. I'm asking the

Lord that you change your family, your community, and your city, and that you will shift into all the new things that God has for you.

There may be someone who is reading this book who doesn't know Jesus. It would be a great day to receive Him as your Savior. Believe that He died on the cross for you. Open your life to partnership with Him, to walk with Him by faith on a great journey, a wonderful journey.

Perhaps God is really speaking to your heart about actually giving yourself to the work of the Lord. God is not unrighteous to forget your work of love; He wants you to minister to His people and continually minister to the people you meet.

Whatever is in your hand, take it and use it to make Jesus known to people, even if it's just a simple act of kindness in some way. Use it to make manifest the reality of God's love.

Now is the time to grow, to step into all God has for you.

It is time to get **STRONGER!**

www.ingramcontent.com/pod-product-compliance
Lightning Source LLC
Chambersburg PA
CBHW061328040426
42444CB00011B/2818